SCALES OVER CHORDS

How to improvise . . . and never play bad notes!

WRITTEN & PRODUCED BY:

WILBUR M. SAVIDGE • RANDY LEE VRADENBURG

SCALES OVER CHORDS
How to improvise . . . and never play bad notes!

WRITTEN & PRODUCED BY:

WILBUR M. SAVIDGE • RANDY LEE VRADENBURG

SECOND EDITION

© Copyright 1994 by Praxis Music Publications, Inc.
International Copyright Secured
Printed in the United States of America

Exclusive Publication Rights:
Praxis Music Publications, Inc.

ISBN 1-884848-05-2

CREDITS:

Graphic Design – Cover / Text	Wilbur M. Savidge
Production Supervision	Randy Lee Vradenburg
Photography	Isac Photo Design
Composition	TEAM Graphix, Inc.
/ Color Separations	European Color Scan, Inc.

COVER GUITAR:

Fender Stratacaster – Serial #23 of 100

The Story of "The Red Strat"

The red Stratacaster photographed for the cover of this book was chosen for its unique beauty and style and bares a mark in demonstration of its ruggedness. The picture you see is the result of our second photographer. During the first photo session, the camera, mounted on a balcony, came loose and fell some ten feet, impacting the instrument, shattering the camera and lens. The damage to the guitar was confined to a direct hit on the guitar's jack plate, placing a "ding" in the top. This resulted in months of controversy, a struggle between the photographer, an insurance company and the instrument's owner (a music store). Eventually, all ended well. A new photographer was used and Randy Lee Vradenburg is now the proud owner of this beautiful instrument.

A PRODUCT OF:

PRAXIS MUSIC PUBLICATIONS, INC.
Bedford, Texas 76021

PERSONAL COMMENTS

Randy Lee Vradenburg   **Wilbur M. Savidge**

Back in 1966, while working on the Guitar Phonics albums, my mentor, Chet Atkins, stated in all his wisdom that *"he was the picker, I was the teacher!"* This has proven to be a profound truth, for I have found that *"if I can understand it, I can teach it"*. I have taught thousands of students, and authored six guitar educational books which are successful enough that I now spend most of my time running a business; and with this book came the time to make allowances for my duties as president of a publishing company. It is therefore with pleasure, I introduce to you a gentleman, a friend of 20 years and a man with demonstrated abilities as a guitarist and teacher. Randy Lee Vradenburg began his musical career at age 10, and through hard work and dedication, has developed into a premier performer, teacher and band leader. He is currently busy playing in and producing jingles, demos and albums. He is an outstanding teacher and has worked diligently to improve teaching techniques to make learning the guitar fun and exciting. I asked Randy to co-author this book for I knew he had the experience, patience and thoughtfulness to be of immeasurable assistance. Randy also performs all the lead guitar work on the optional Audio Companion cassette tape, and the BandJam Video.

– BILL SAVIDGE, Publisher

< 2 >

TABLE OF CONTENTS

Personal Comments 2
Table of Contents 3
Introduction 4
Rules of Improvisation 5
Section One: Basic Improvisational Theory 6
Creating Music 7
Types of Intervals 8
Types of Scales 9
Chromatic Scales 10
Playing Chromatic Scales 11
The Guitar Fingerboard 13
The Major Diatonic Scale 15
The Scale in Theoretical Form 17
Reading Key Signatures 19
Street Smarts Review 21
Section Two: Scale Pattern Development 22
The Diatonic Scale–Five Scale Patterns 23
Five Chord Forms 24
Form *C* Pattern 25
Form *A* Pattern 27
Form *G* Pattern 28
Form *E* Pattern 29
Form *D* Pattern 30
The *C A G E D* Sequence of Chords 31
Scale Pattern Development 33
Form *C* Pattern 34
Form *A* Pattern 35
Form *G* Pattern 36
Form *E* Pattern 37
Form *D* Pattern 38
Street Smarts Review 39
Section Three: Chord Harmony Study 40
Harmonizing the Major Scale 41
Relationship of Chords 43
Primary Chords 45
Extended Dominant Seventh Chords 46
Dominant Seventh Chords
    & the Mixolydian Scale 47
Arpeggios 49
C Form Triads 49
A Form Triads 51
G Form Triads 53
E Form Triads 55
D Form Triads 57
Street Smarts Review 59
Section Four: Modal Playing 60
Modes–The Scales of Improvisation 61
Modes–Derived From Major Scales 63
Modes–Form One *C* Scale Pattern 65
Dorian Mode 66
Phrygian Mode 67
Lydian Mode 68
Mixolydian Mode 69
Aeolian Mode 70
Locrian Mode 71
Modes–Form Two *A* Scale Pattern
Dorian Mode 72
Phrygian Mode 73
Lydian Mode 74
Mixolydian Mode 75
Aeolian Mode 76
Locrian Mode 77
Modes–Form Three *G* Scale Pattern
Dorian Mode 78

Phrygian Mode 79
Lydian Mode 80
Mixolydian Mode 81
Aeolian Mode 82
Locrian Mode 83
Modes–Form Four *E* Scale Pattern
Dorian Mode 84
Phrygian Mode 85
Lydian Mode 86
Mixolydian Mode 87
Aeolian Mode 88
Locrian Mode 89
Modes–Form Five *D* Scale Pattern
Dorian Mode 90
Phrygian Mode 91
Lydian Mode 92
Mixolydian Mode 93
Aeolian Mode 94
Locrian Mode 95
Modal Index 96
Street Smarts Review 97
Section Five: Triadic Improvisation 98
Rules of Triadic Improvisation 99
Triadic Harmonization Chart 100
Modal Playing 101
Improvising Over Major Chords 102
Improvising Over Diatonic Minor Chords 103
Key Centers 105
C Scale–Seven Chords 106
Identifying Chord Groups 107
IV-V-I Progression 108
ii-V-I Progression 109
Study Exercise 57 110
Vi-IV-V-I Progression 111
Study Exercise 58 112
Study Exercise 59 114
Study Exercise 60 116
Study Exercise 61 118
Street Smarts Review 119
Section Six: Tools of Creative Improvisation 120
Creative Tools 121
Study Exercise 62 122
Study Exercise 63 124
Elements of Improvisation 125
Time Signatures 126
Rock Song 128
Country Song 130
Blues Song 132
Jazz Song 134
Chord Diagrams 135
Chord Diagrams 136
Chord Diagrams 137
Chord Diagrams 138
Chord Diagrams 139
Rules of Modal Harmony (Review) 140
C & *G* Harmonization Chart 141
D & *A* Harmonization Chart 142
E & *F* Harmonization Chart 143
Teacher's Section 144
Blank Chord Diagrams 146-149
Two Measure Staff Sheets 150-152
Four Measure Staff Sheets 153-154
Five Measure Staff Sheets 155-156
Notes 157-159

INTRODUCTION

SCALES OVER CHORDS

"Improvisation, is the spontaneous creation of a rhythmic melodic line over a group of chords. It involves applied knowledge and human creativity. It is a way of expressing one-self musically, through the instrument."

– Tradic Improvisation: Wilbur M. Savidge.

◊ All guitarists desire to create music, to play in a band, jam with friends, participate in a recording session, or just be able to express themselves in their living room. Lacking a working knowledge of scales, modes and how they play over chord progressions will certainly hinder these aspirations. It is the purpose of this book to teach you how to play a solo with forethought and knowledge utilizing a "street smarts" approach to theory. Boring and traditional methods of teaching theory has been avoided. Everything we show you will be presented in easy to follow steps which allow you to build upon the knowledge you already possess. This book will open the doors for the beginner, and provide the knowledge and tools required in order to begin the journey into improvisation. The advanced player will find new insights into how to be more creative, and how to play new and more complex lead lines.

◊ You will find in this book new and exciting information. You will be given examples, then shown how to use the information your way. We also encourage you to work with the Audio Companion cassette tape (sold separately), for it not only offers you the opportunity to hear examples played on the guitar, the audio tape presents a special feature – you can play along with a band! You can experiment with all the knowledge you obtain from you studies with this book, you can try new ideas, practice old tricks, all in the environment of having your own band to back you up. Even better, we provide a truly new concept, BANDJAM, a 45-minute video with which you can actually see the examples demonstrated, and then stand in front of a band the and show your stuff! Ask your music dealer for a demonstration of this remarkable Entertainment/Educational Video. (BANDJAM Video sold separately).

Mission Statement

A. To enable you to choose the correct scale (mode) that will play over a given chord progression, so you may always play correct notes.

B. To teach you how to look at a chord progression and identify the key in which the song is written.

C. To teach you how to create riffs, motifs and lead lines that are correct (no bad notes) and fit the rhythm structure of the music, so you will play with competence and flair.

E. To give you playing experience in a variety of musical styles. (Requires the Audio Companion.)

RULES OF IMPROVISATION

To improvise successfully, one must possess sufficient knowledge of music theory (how things work) to establish a working perimeter. Once we can apply a few rules of what will work, we can then use our intuitive ability to improvise, to create music "on the fly".

We are going to teach you how to play scales over chords. Why? Because chords are built from scale tones! Chords are the results of harmonizing a scale, placing notes in intervals of thirds, fourths, fifths, etc. on top of each other. By playing notes of the scale of which the chord is constructed, you will learn to relate scales and chords together. When the proper scale is played over a given chord progression, we will not play any bad notes.

What are the key elements you must understand and apply correctly in order to improvise?

1. You must understand the theory of intervals, scales, modes, chords, and arpeggios.

2. You must know and be able to play scales in five patterns on the fingerboard.

3. You must have a "developed" ear; the acquired ability to distinguish tones, intervals, and chord harmony.

4. You must understand the principle rhythm structure of various types of music: Jazz, Blues, Country, Pop, etc.,.

5. You must know how to determine "Key Centers" within a chord progression.

6. You must develop the technique to to create riffs, motifs, lead lines, and how to connect them together.

Improvisation goes beyond sight reading, and while we encourage you to develop this ability, it is the purpose of this book to provide you with the knowledge to think intelligently and play correctly over any given chord progression. Study all examples and make sure you understand the principals explained, so you may play and create solos with ease and skill.

How to Use This Book

"Scales Over Chords," is divided into 6 sections. Each section focuses on one element of improvisation. There are no short cuts. If you wish to succeed, study, assimilate and learn to use the information presented in each section. As a complete text, the knowledge in this book provides a comprehensive study of this fascinating subject.

< 5 >

BASIC IMPROVISATIONAL THEORY

Improvisational playing is playing by ear and using applied knowledge to create music "on the fly". This requires a working knowledge of how music works. This section teaches the rudiments of music theory, not sight reading, just an explanation of how the elements of music fit together. If this information is unfamiliar, please take the time necessary to learn the concepts presented.

> ### BEGIN WITH
> ### YOUR STRENGHTS
>
> *Start with what you can now do. Perfect it. Focus on what you do best and success will follow.*

< 6 >

BASIC IMPROVISATIONAL THEORY

CREATING MUSIC

Creating music is about organizing pitch and developing melodies that are interesting and pleasant to the ear. This book focuses specifically on single-note improvisation and how to connect solo ideas into long, smooth, uninterrupted lines. Our objective is to offer ways you can create solo lines over established chord progression and to know how to use scales that are appropriate to the musical setting.

The Tools We Use Are: **INTERVALS, SCALES, CHORDS, AND ARPEGGIOS**.

DEFINITIONS

INTERVALS:

An Interval is the difference in pitch between any two notes measured in whole and half-steps. The lower tone is considered the Root or Tonic, the upper tone is the INTERVAL.

SCALES:

All scales are a predetermined pattern of notes arranged in steps and half-steps (whole tones and half tones). A whole step is the distance of two frets on the guitar. Scales are depicted on the staff by notes written in ascending or descending order.

CHORDS:

A chord is the simultaneous sounding of three (or more) tones called a triad. There are four types of chords and many variations of each. We have Major, Minor, Augmented, and Diminished chords, plus variations such as 6ths, 7ths, 9ths, 11th, and 13ths. Chords may also utilize altered tones such as: b5th and #9th.

ARPEGGIOS:

An arpeggio is some or all notes of a chord played one note at a time.

< 7 >

BASIC IMPROVISATIONAL THEORY

TYPES OF INTERVALS

When two tones of different pitch are played in succession, it is called a MELODIC INTERVAL. When two tones are played together (as in a chord), it is called an HARMONIC INTERVAL.

Intervals are identified by their position in the scale. They are named according to their distance from the tonic note.

PRIME or UNISON INTERVAL
The first interval is called the PRIME of UNISON interval – two notes of the same letter- two tones of the same pitch.

PERFECT INTERVALS
The UNISON, FOURTH, FIFTH, and OCTAVE are called PERFECT intervals because they remain constant from key to key.

MINOR INTERVALS
When notes of a Major interval are brought closer together, we have a MINOR interval. This may be accomplished by lowering the upper tone, one half-step or raising the lower tone a half-step. The second, third, sixth and seventh intervals may be played as MINOR INTERVALS.

DIMINISHED INTERVALS
The DIMINISHED interval is obtained by bringing a PERFECT interval or a MINOR interval one half-step closer.

AUGMENTED INTERVALS
When the interval between two tones is EXPANDED, the interval is called AUGMENTED. This applies to both the Major and Perfect intervals. Each of these become augmented by raising the upper note one half-step, or lowering the lower tone one half-step.

TRITONE INTERVAL
The interval between the fourth and fifth is called the TRITONE. Because of the "enharmonic" spelling, the Tritone interval may be called either an "augmented' fourth, or a "diminished" fifth.

INTERVALS IN WRITTEN FORM

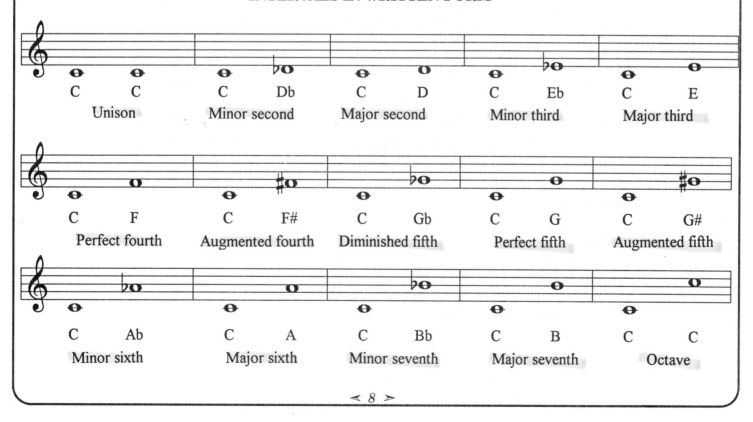

BASIC IMPROVISATIONAL THEORY

TYPES OF SCALES

All music is based on the proven scientific fact that the notes we use to create music have fixed rates of vibration which are mathematically related to one another. Each note has a pitch which we can produce vocally or with a musical instrument. These notes, when played in fixed patterns, are called scales.

When we have two notes of the same name, but one of different pitch, one written higher than the other and vice versa, they are said to be an OCTAVE apart. It is important to realize that an octave does not consist of 13 tones, but is the 13th note above the first of a series of 12 successive notes.

In our study of improvisation we will explore the usage of the following scales: *Chromatic Scale, Diatonic Major Scale* and is its derivative scales, *called Modes.*

CHROMATIC SCALE

ILLUSTRATION ONE

The interval sequence of notes upon which all scales are built is called a CHROMATIC SCALE. The chromatic scale is one octave divided into 12 tones, called half-steps.

ILLUSTRATION TWO

Since we have 12 notes in music (not counting their enharmonic names), we have 12 Chromatic Scales, each starting on a different note of the scale. This is the basis of establishing our musical KEYS. If the first note of the scale is the note A, we would have the "A chromatic Scale".

ILLUSTRATION THREE

The black and white piano keyboard presents the chromatic scale in a clear, visual way that is not as obvious on the guitar fingerboard. The keys of the piano keyboard represent one Chromatic Scale repeating itself in higher and higher octaves with the lowest octave on the left of the keyboard. The distance between each key, black or white, is the distance of a half-step.

The division of the chromatic scale into 12 tones (half-steps), is accomplished on the guitar neck by the placement of the fingerboard frets. The distance between each fret is called a half-step. An INTERVAL is the distance between two frets, two notes.

< 9 >

CHROMATIC SCALES

ILLUSTRATION ONE

THE CHROMATIC SCALE

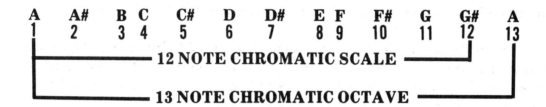

ILLUSTRATION TWO

12 CHROMATIC SCALES

A A# B C C# D D# E F F# G G# A
A# B C C# D D# E F F# G G# A A#
B C C# D D# E F F# G G# A A# B
C C# D D# E F F# G G# A A# B C
C# D D# E F F# G G# A A# B C C#
D D# E F F# G G# A A# B C C# D
D# E F F# G G# A A# B C C# D D#
E F f # G G# A A# B C C# D D# E
F F# G G# A A# B C C# D D# E F
F# G G# A A# B C C# D D# E F F#
G G# A A# B C C# D D# E F F# G
G# A A# B C C# D D# E F F# G G#

ILLUSTRATION THREE

THE PIANO KEYBOARD – A CONTINUOUS CHROMATIC SCALE

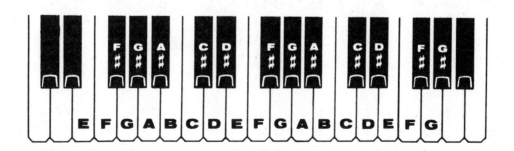

PLAYING CHROMATIC SCALES

Chromatic scale exercises offer an ideal way of developing independent left-hand finger movement. Practicing chromatic scales in ascending and descend order over the entire length of the fingerboard develops the lateral ability to play single line- one string melodies.

ILLUSTRATION ONE

Linear Movement – One String

The following exercises commence on the first fret of the first string. Ascending order: Play four notes (one finger for each note), then shift and play the fifth note with the first finger. Descending order: Commencing with the fourth finger on the 13th fret, again use one finger for each fret, shift and continue the scale. Practice this fingering excise on each string.

ILLUSTRATION TWO

A Movable Six Strings Position

An excellent technique builder, this ascending 'movable' chromatic scale position, shifts back one fret as you play across each string (except the movement across the third string – the tuning thing, a third interval between the *G* and *B* strings, all other strings are tuned a fourth interval apart). Proficiency will require practice as there is a tendency to get lost when making the shifts.

ILLUSTRATION THREE

A Movable Position – Six Strings

Again, an excellent left-hand development exercise, all notes are placed (in ascending order), forward of the first finger which acts as a barr. Notice that the fourth finger plays two notes. Develop the stretch required (a five finger reach), so a forward movement of the left hand is not required.

STREET SMARTS

Chromatic scales provide a great connecting link between scales and "licks" played at different positions on the fingerboard. Also, they may be use to connect arpeggios and large interval skips.

< 11 >

CHROMATIC SCALES

ILLUSTRATION ONE
Linear Movement

Put on first string

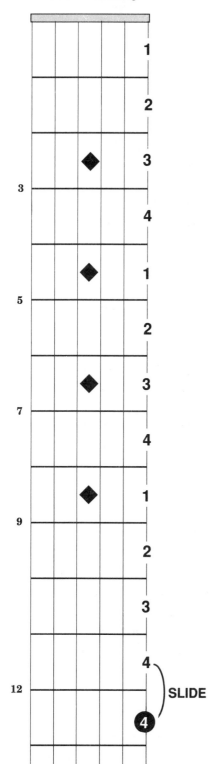

ILLUSTRATION TWO
Moveable Six-String Position

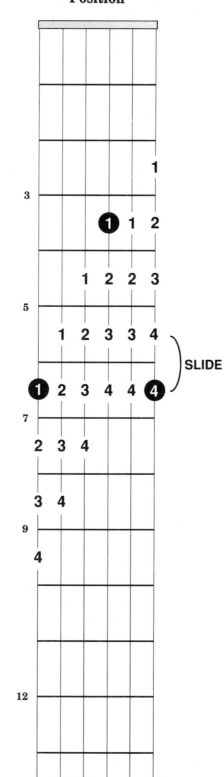

ILLUSTRATION THREE
Moveable Six-String Position

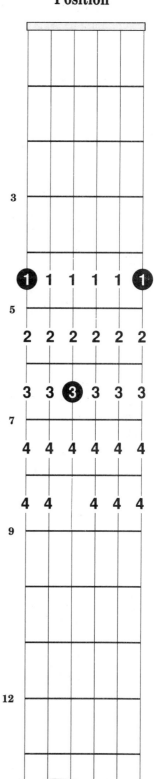

THE GUITAR FINGERBOARD

The six strings of the guitar make up six chromatic scales. Each scale starts on the note in the chromatic scale upon which the guitar string is tuned and continues up the neck, ascending in pitch until the tone is repeated again at the 12th fret. Twelve frets plus the open string tone equals one octave.

In our study, it is important to fully understand the tonal relationship of chromatic scale notes, for the chromatic scale includes every pitch within an octave. It is upon the chromatic scale we build the more simplistic scales used in establishing our musical keys: the Diatonic Major and Minor Scales. Remember: The chromatic scale simply represents, in alphabetical order, our interval system of notes.

It is important to memorize the fingerboard. It can be a formidable task. However, if you start by learning the names of the open strings, the educational process can be greatly simplified by visualizing a chromatic scale in your head.

SIX CHROMATIC SCALES

THE
COMPLETE
GUITAR FINGER BOARD

(12 FRETS PLUS THE OPEN STRINGS)

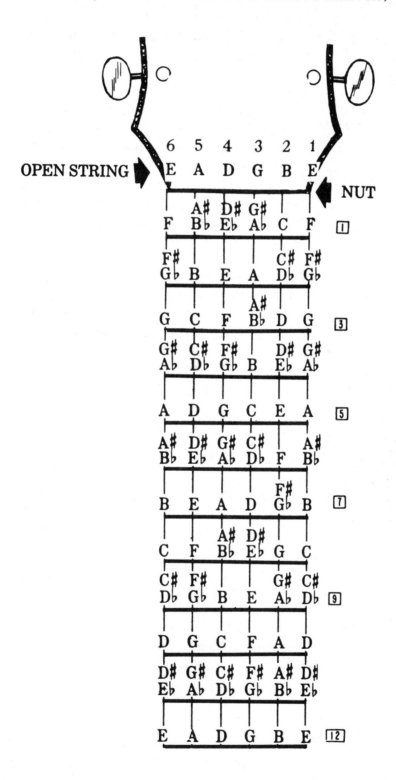

BASIC IMPROVISATIONAL THEORY

THE MAJOR DIATONIC SCALE

Most modern music is not written with chromatic scales, but with a more manageable, pleasant-sounding, eight note scale called a DIATONIC SCALE. The Diatonic Major Scale with its familiar Do-Re-Mi-Fa-So-La-Ti-Do sound, Illustration Three, is the scale used to create the vast majority of the music guitarists encounter daily. It is from the Diatonic Major Scale that the minor, the pentatonic, and our modal system of scales originate. To understand the art of improvisation, we must therefore fully understand the step pattern (the degree name and number) of the diatonic scale and be able to play scales in five patterns on the fingerboard.

ILLUSTRATION ONE

The Major Diatonic Scale is a predetermined pattern of eight notes arranged in five whole steps (whole tones) and two half-steps (semi-tones). A half-step is the distance of one fret on the guitar: a whole step is the distance of two frets. In other words, a Major Diatonic Scale is a succession of tones arranged in a fixed step, half-step pattern. The distance between notes remains constant and the interval between notes is fixed and will not change even if the music is played in another key. In this manner, we recognize a song and can hum the melody, regardless of the key (pitch) in which is performed, thus making it possible to transpose a piece of music to different keys.

A diatonic scale may be built commencing on any of the twelve notes of the chromatic scale. Thus, we have twelve major scales called KEYS, each a different pitch. The sound of the Major Diatonic Scale is due to the placement of the half-steps between the 3rd and 4th notes and between the 7th and 8th notes. The resulting two-tone (step, step), interval between the 1st and 3rd notes create the scales major characteristic. (A lowered third, step half-step, creates a minor sound).

ILLUSTRATION TWO

C SCALE NOTES ON THE GUITAR FINGERBOARD
Experiment with the step, step, half-step, step, step, step, half-step principle on the guitar. Start at any fret and walk up the fingerboard using the correct step, half-step patterns. Your ending note should always be the same letter name as your starting tone. In playing the scale pattern, use four fingers. Always start the pattern with your first finger on the first note.

ILLUSTRATION THREE

DEGREES OF THE SCALE
Each step of the Diatonic Scale may be indicted by Roman numerals. This designation is used commonly in theory books. Each degree also has a proper theoretical name. The terms Tonic, Subdominant, and Dominant are also used to describe the three primary chord of each Key.

ILLUSTRATION FOUR

C MAJOR DIATONIC SCALE - WRITTEN FORM
This illustration represents the C Major scale as it appears in written form.

< 15 >

DIATONIC SCALE

THE MAJOR DIATONIC SCALE:
7 NOTES

THE MAJOR DIATONIC OCTAVE:
13 NOTES

ILLUSTRATION ONE — Key of *C*

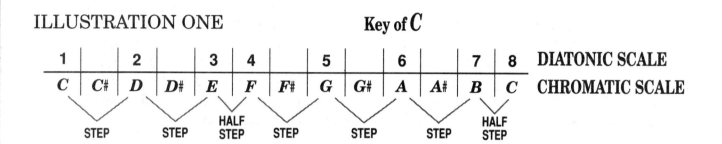

ILLUSTRATION TWO — Notes on the Fingerboard — *C* Scale = Step, Step, Half Step

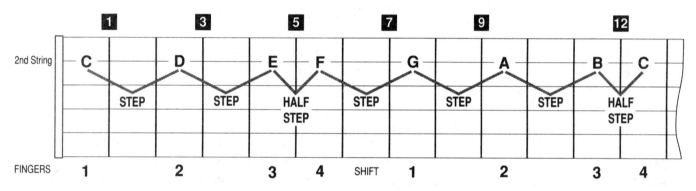

ILLUSTRATION THREE — Degrees of the Scale

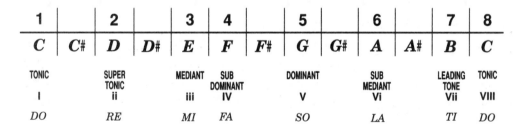

ILLUSTRATION FOUR — *C* Diatonic Scale in Written Form

< 16 >

BASIC IMPROVISATIONAL THEORY

THE SCALE IN THEORETICAL FORM

ILLUSTRATION ONE

ALPHABETICAL NAMES

Each Diatonic Scale will have a different group of letters (notes) and a different arrangement and number of sharps or flats. In our example, the *C Major* Scale- *C D EF G A BC*, we do not have any sharps or flats, called accidentals. The *C* diatonic scale is called the NATURAL SCALE.

SCALE DEGREES

Each note of the scale is called a DEGREE, and may be indicted by ARABIC Numerals: 1 2 3 4 5 6 7 8. Each degree may also be indicated by ROMAN Numerals. The usage of Roman Numerals is common in chord theory studies. A capitol Roman number (II) indicates major chords. Small letters (i i) represents minor chords.

THE DO RE MI SYSTEM

The Do Re Mi system of identifying scale degrees was developed as an educational aid in teaching vocalists to 'sing' notes on pitch, Do, being the first note of a diatonic scale, the Tonic note.

THEORETICAL FORM

The correct theoretical name for each degree of the scale (Tonic, Super Tonic, Mediant, Subdominant, Dominant, Submediant, Leading Tone, Tonic, is commonly used in chord theory studies.

INTERVALS

An Interval is the distance between two tones.

ILLUSTRATION TWO

The Diatonic Scale, eight notes, can be continued on in higher or lower sequence called OCTAVES. It is permissible to continue counting numerically – 9 10 11 12 13 14 15 – to determine the next octave. The first and eighth notes are the same alphabetically. When building "extended" chords, 9th, 11th, 13th, this continuation of the scale is utilized to determine the names these additional notes.

STREET SMARTS

The Diatonic Scale is the "Mother Scale" of improvisation. You must be able to create diatonic scales from SCRATCH, to be able to locate the Key note, the Tonic, and walk the step / half-step pattern of the diatonic scale either in a linear-straight-line movement, or by using a zig-zag movement across the neck, creating the proper step pattern of a diatonic scale in any given key. With just a little practice, you will be able, instinctively, to walk the fingerboard, correctly playing all the notes of any given key. And as you will see, by memorizing the eight step numbers you will be able to play all the scales used in the art of improvisation.

< 17 >

THE DIATONIC SCALE

THEORETICAL FORM

ILLUSTRATION ONE

THE C MAJOR DIATONIC SCALE

ALPHABETICAL	C	D	E	F	G	A	B	C
ARABIC	1	2	3	4	5	6	7	8
ROMAN	I	ii	iii	1V	V	Vi	Vii	VIII
SOL-FA	DO	RE	MI	FA	SOL	LA	TI	DO
THEORETICAL	TONIC	SUPER TONIC	MEDIANT	SUB DOM	DOMINANT	SUB MEDIANT	LEADING TONE	TONIC
INTERVALS	PERFECT PRIME	MAJOR SECOND	MAJOR THIRD	PERFECT FOURTH	PERFECT FIFTH	MAJOR SIXTH	MAJOR SEVENTH	PERFECT OCTAVE
ABBREVIATIONS	(P.P.)	(Ma 2)	(Ma 3)	(P. 4)	(P. 5)	(Ma 6)	(Ma 7)	(P. 8)

ILLUSTRATION TWO

THE DIATONIC SCALE EXTENDED TWO OCTAVES

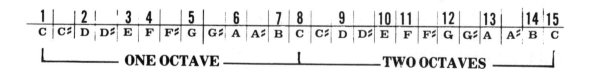

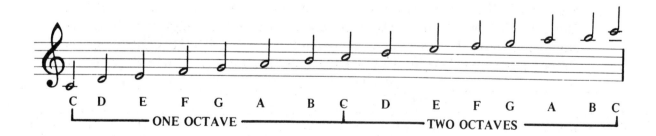

< 18 >

BASIC IMPROVISATIONAL THEORY

READING KEY SIGNATURES

A piece of music is written in a particular KEY which defines the PITCH or TONALITY of the scale in which the music is written. We indicate the key (pitch) by a device called the KEY SIGNATURE. The purpose of the key signature is to indicate the sharps or flats that belong in each individual scale. It eases the eye by avoiding the placing of sharps or flats against particular notes every time they occur in the arrangement. We write the key signature simply by placing the appropriate number of sharps (Illustration One) or flats (Illustration Two) on the music staff after the clef sign and before the time signature. They effect all designated notes appearing in the arrangement.

The Circle of Fifths

As previously explained, key signatures are used to establish keys and to indicate what notes must be raised or lowered in order to maintain the step, half-step pattern that establishes the major diatonic scale.

The key of *C Major* is the simplest of our scales. Commencing on the note *C*, the diatonic step, half-step pattern produces a scale without sharps or flats. The method by which the placement of accidentals occurs follows a very simplistic theme and is called the Circle of Fifths.

The Circle of Fifths is a visual device that shows the relationship between the Tonic (1), and the Sub-dominant (4), and Dominant (5) notes within a diatonic scale. It presents in logical order the addition of required accidentals as keys of different pitch are created. The Circle of Fifths is based upon two concepts.

Dominant Direction- (5ths) Sharps

Starting with the key of *C*, sharp keys are created by counting up an interval of a fifth (*CDEFG*) The new key is *G Major*. The note *G* is the fifth note in the *C* scale. In order to maintain the proper step, half-step pattern, the seventh note of the new scale (*G*) has been raised a half-step, creating one sharp note in the *G* scale (*F sharp*).

Sub-dominant Direction- (4ths) Flats

Starting with the key of *C*, flat keys are created by counting up an interval of a fourth (*CDEF*). The new key is *F Major*. The note F is the fourth note in the *C* Scale. In order to maintain the proper step, half-step pattern, the seventh note has been lowered a half step, creating one flat in the *F* scale (*Bb*).

KEY SIGNATURES

ILLUSTRATION ONE

SHARP KEYS circle of 5ths

C

G

D

A

E

B

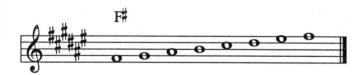

F#

ILLUSTRATION TWO

FLAT KEYS circle of 4ths

C

F

B♭

E♭

A♭

D♭

G♭

C♭

C#

< 20 >

BASIC IMPROVISATIONAL THEORY

section one

STREET SMARTS REVIEW

─── *STREET SMARTS* ───

Chromatic scales provide a great connecting links between scales and "licks", played at different positions on the fingerboard. They may also be used to connect arpeggios and large interval skips.

─── *Page 11* ───

─── *STREET SMARTS* ───

Learn to recognize octaves (F to F as an example). Remember, all scales are played between octaves.

─── *Page 13* ───

─── *STREET SMARTS* ───

The Diatonic Scale is the "Mother Scale" of improvisation. You must be able to create diatonic scales from SCRATCH, to be able to locate the Key note, the Tonic, and walk the step/half-step pattern of the diatonic scale either in a linear-straight-line movement, or by using a zig-zag movement across the neck, creating the proper step pattern of a diatonic scale in any given key.

With just a little practice, you will be able to instrinctively walk the fingerboard, correctly playing all the notes of any given key. And as you will see, by memorizing the eight-step numbers you will be able to play all the scales used in the art of improvisation.

─── *Page 17* ───

─── *STREET SMARTS* ───

It is extremely important for you to develop the ability to look at key signatures, the placement and number of sharps or flats; and we know what key in which you are to play.

Remember: *The key signature sets the key – the scale. The scale determines the chords and generally provides all the tools required in order to play solos and riffs.*

─── *Page 19* ───

< 21 >

SCALE PATTERN DEVELOPMENT

Notes do not appear at random on the fingerboard. Every aspect of music, as applied to the guitar, is systematic and predictable. Notes may be organized into various types of scales, which provide order, and patterns can be developed. On the following pages, we explore the usage of five scale patterns. Each pattern is movable throughout the range of the fingerboard. Become an expert on scales, because in them lies the real secret of improvisation.

FOCUS ON YOUR SPECIAL TALENTS

Every strength is a springboard that can propel you on to the next plateau. When confused or in doubt, pick one strength to pursue, master it, then move on!

< 22 >

THE DIATONIC SCALE IN 5 HAND POSITIONS – 5 SCALE PATTERNS

Understanding scale theory is a mental process and easy to grasp, whereas playing a scale is a physical task and takes longer to master. On the guitar, there are countless fingering pattern possibilities for any given scale, so it is desirable to reduce the options to a few more manageable forms.

There are three ways we can play scales: a LINEAR, lengthwise movement, a ZIG-ZAG movement, and a POSITION. At this time we will concentrate on playing scales in fixed positions. To begin, we must first focus on learning to play the Diatonic Scale in five basic hand positions.

A position encompasses all notes of a given scale placed, normally, within five frets. There are "open positions" – scales played within the first four frets and utilizing notes produced by the open strings (*E A D G B E*), and movable "closed positions", no open string notes, which produce a new key at each fret.

The closed position ascends and descends chromatically moving through the entire twelve notes of music and will produce the notes of 12 keys.

There are several diatonic scale finger patterns in common usage – fingering systems developed by individual guitarists to facilitate their unique style of playing. We are using fingering patterns made popular by the late Los Angeles studio pro, Jack Marshall. These five patterns relate to the five chords forms found in the "open position" – the open chords: *C, A, G, E* and *D*. This system of one scale fingering pattern for each chord form is used by guitarists Howard Roberts, Barney Kessel, and Herb Ellis.

The five patterns divide the fingerboard into smaller more manageable areas of learning, but put them end to end, they cover the entire range of the fingerboard. When we are able to visualize the entire fingerboard as a whole, fingering becomes a personal preference.

ILLUSTRATION ONE

Open Chord Forms
Here we present the five chords upon which the five scale patterns are constructed. Black triangles indicted the Tonic note(s) of each chord.

ILLUSTRATION TWO

Closed Chord Forms
Here we illustrate the "open" chords played as "movable" chords.

PRACTICE TIP
Practice playing the open chord. Then, play the closed form.

STREET SMARTS
*By playing the **fingering pattern** correctly, you have played the **scale** correctly!*

< 23 >

FIVE CHORD FORMS

ILLUSTRATION ONE

OPEN CHORDS

Form One	Form Two	Form Three	Form Four	Form Five
C	*A*	*G*	*E*	*D*

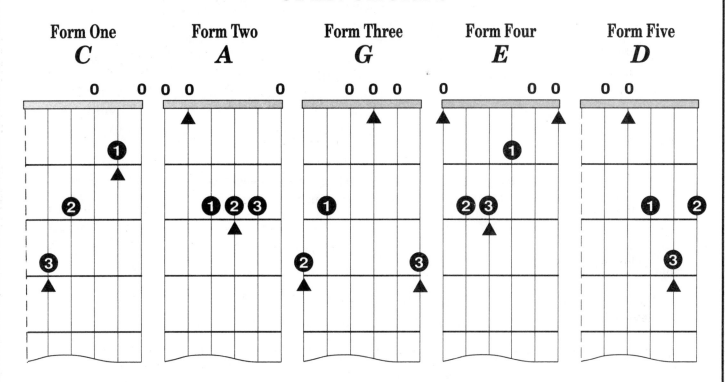

ILLUSTRATION TWO

CLOSED CHORDS (Moveable)

Form One	Form Two	Form Three	Form Four	Form Five

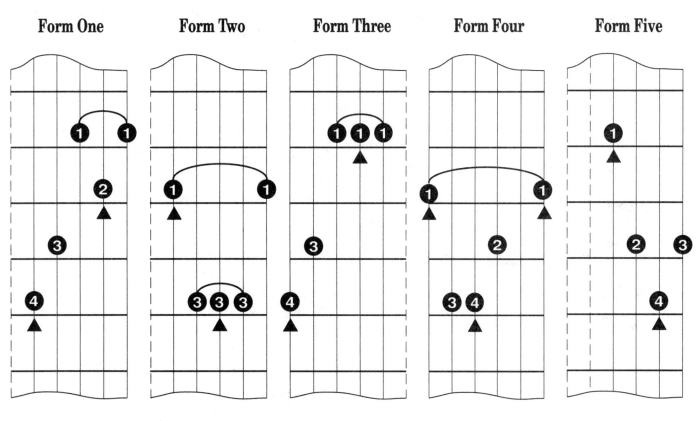

SCALE PATTERN DEVELOPMENT

C SCALE PATTERN – FORM ONE

There are five basic barr chord forms in common usage, and since most guitarists have a working knowledge of barr chords and how each ascends and descends chromatically, it becomes quite easy to know scales in all 12 keys. Each scale pattern overlays its respective chord form, (all notes of the chord triad are within the scale), therefore chord harmony and arpeggio playing is locked in with the scale. We mark the Tonic note of the pattern and chord with a black triangle so you may know upon which string they receive their name. Remember: Since each scale pattern moves through the entire range of the fingerboard, mastering one finger pattern actually provides you with the skill to play in all twelve keys. A lick or solo played in one key may be played in any key without changing the fingering that produced the notes.

Example: At the fifth fret we can play an *A Major* barr chord. The scale form that produces the *A* chord will be an *A* diatonic scale. Play the same chord form at the eighth fret, we have a *C Major* chord. The scale will now be a *C* diatonic scale.

Each scale pattern is a fixed position on the fingerboard. Develop the "stretch" required to properly finger each scale. This requires a one-finger-per-fret approach. The correct fingering is indicated on the TAB charts by small encircled numbers. In some of the patterns you need to reach one fret above or below the basic position, a five fret reach. We begin each pattern with the lowest note available within the range of the pattern. The Tonic note is marked with a black triangle.

NOTE: Proper finger articulation is the prerequisite for the fluent execution of scales. Experiment with all five scale patterns. It is our belief that you should strive to master the fingerings indicated for each pattern.

ILLUSTRATION ONE Open pattern

This is the first of our five open scale patterns. It encompasses within the open position, all notes of the *C Major* Scale. It is called the *C* pattern because it overlays the open string *C* chord form.

ILLUSTRATION TWO Closed "movable" pattern

This is the first of our five closed scale patterns. It encompasses all notes of the scale associated with the movable *C* chord form. This pattern can be played in higher or lower positions on the fingerboard. The Tonic note (the name of the scale) is located on both the fifth and second strings. We can simply state: The Tonic note slides up and down on the chromatic scale of the string upon which the Tonic note is located. The Tonic note establishes the Key or name of the scale at each fret. The pattern correctly produces the proper sharp or flat notes common to the that scale.

> ## PRACTICE TIP
> Play the chord, then play the scale. Develop the ability to move with ease between the chord and scale. Practice all notes in each position and learn to play above and below the octave notes in each scale pattern.

< 25 >

C SCALE PATTERN – FORM ONE

ILLUSTRATION ONE ② *ROCK BEAT TEMPO 155*

OPEN PATTERN

C SCALE

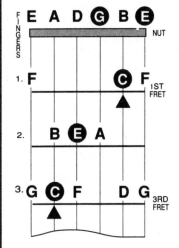

C MAJOR SCALE (Open)

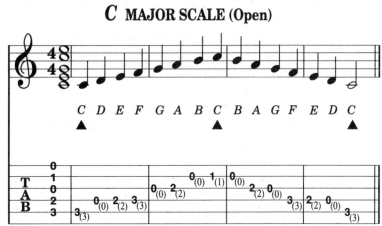

C CHORD: *C E G* TRIAD

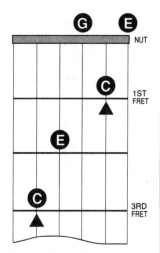

ILLUSTRATION TWO ③ *ROCK BEAT TEMPO 155*

CLOSED "MOVEABLE" PATTERN

D SCALE

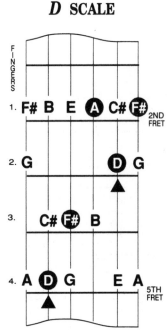

D MAJOR SCALE (Moveable)

D CHORD: *D F# A* TRIAD

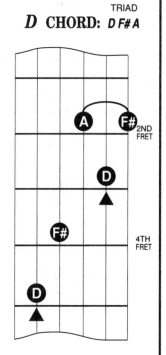

< 26 >

3/2/96

ILLUSTRATION ONE (4) ROCK BEAT TEMPO 155

OPEN PATTERN

This is the second of our five open scale patterns. It encompasses, within the open position, all notes of the A Major scale. It is called the A pattern, because it overlays the open string A chord form.

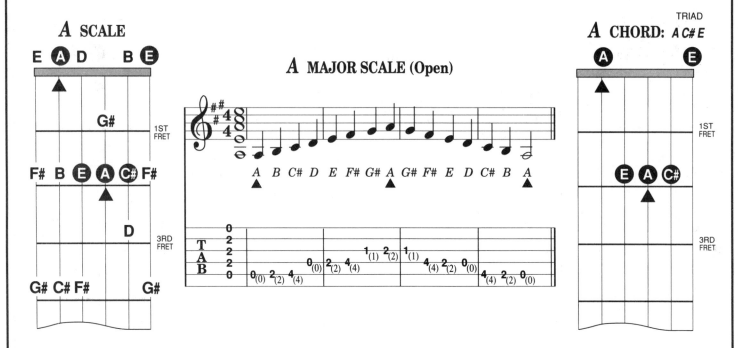

A SCALE

A MAJOR SCALE (Open)

A CHORD: A C# E

ILLUSTRATION TWO (5) ROCK BEAT TEMPO 155

CLOSED "MOVEABLE" PATTERN

This is the second of our five closed scale patterns. It encompasses all notes of the scale associated with the moveable A chord form. The Tonic note (name of the scale), is located on the fifth and third strings. The Tonic note establishes the Key or name of the scale at each fret.

C SCALE

C MAJOR SCALE (Moveable)

C CHORD: C E G

< 27 >

G SCALE PATTERN - FORM THREE

ILLUSTRATION ONE ⑥ ROCK BEAT TEMPO 155

OPEN PATTERN

This is the third of our five open scale patterns. It encompasses, within the open position, all notes of the *G* Major scale. It is called the *G* pattern, because it overlays the open string *G* chord form.

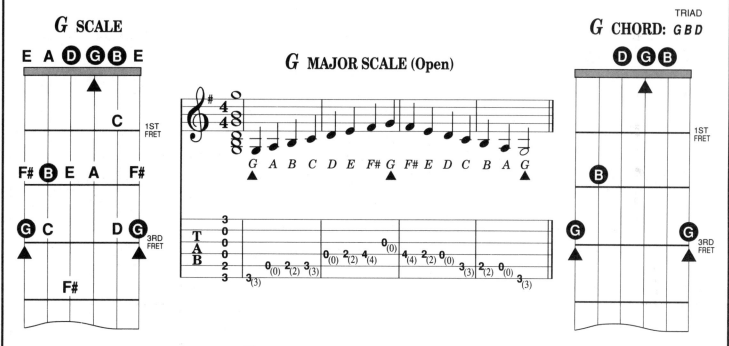

G SCALE

G MAJOR SCALE (Open)

G CHORD: *G B D*

ILLUSTRATION TWO ⑦ ROCK BEAT TEMPO 155

CLOSED "MOVEABLE" PATTERN

This is the third of our five closed scale patterns. It encompasses all notes of the scale associated with the moveable G chord form. The Tonic note (name of the scale), is located on the sixth, third and first strings. The Tonic note establishes the Key or name of the scale at each fret.

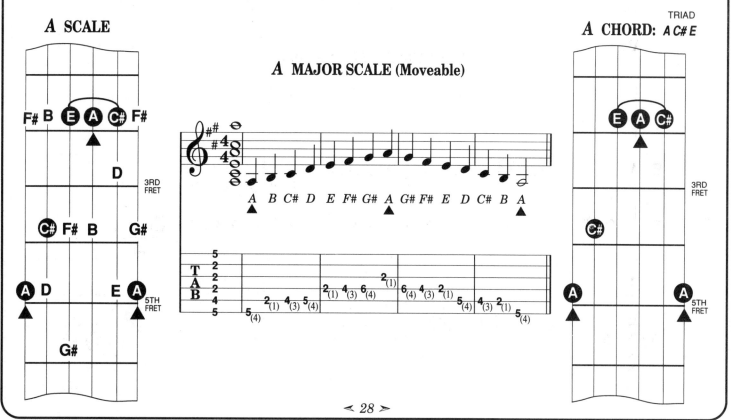

A SCALE

A MAJOR SCALE (Moveable)

A CHORD: *A C# E*

< 28 >

E SCALE PATTERN – FORM FOUR

ILLUSTRATION ONE (8) *ROCK BEAT TEMPO 155*

OPEN PATTERN

This is the fourth of our five open scale patterns. It encompasses, within the open position, all notes of the E Major scale. It is called the E pattern, because it overlays the open string E chord form.

E SCALE

E MAJOR SCALE (Open)

E CHORD: *E G# B*

ILLUSTRATION TWO (9) *ROCK BEAT TEMPO 155*

CLOSED "MOVEABLE" PATTERN

This is the fourth of our five closed scale patterns. It encompasses all notes of the scale associated with the moveable E chord form. The Tonic note (name of the scale), is located on the sixth, fourth and first strings. The Tonic note establishes the Key or name of the scale at each fret.

G SCALE

G MAJOR SCALE (Moveable)

G CHORD: *G B D*

< 29 >

D SCALE PATTERN - FORM FIVE

ILLUSTRATION ONE ROCK BEAT TEMPO 155

OPEN PATTERN

This is the fifth of our five open scale patterns. It encompasses, within the open position, all notes of the D Major scale. It is called the D pattern, because it overlays the open string D chord form.

D SCALE

D MAJOR SCALE (Open)

D CHORD: D F# A

ILLUSTRATION TWO ROCK BEAT TEMPO 155

CLOSED "MOVEABLE" PATTERN

This is the fifth of our five closed scale patterns. It encompasses all notes of the scale associated with the moveable D chord form. The Tonic note (name of the scale), is located on the fourth and second strings. The Tonic note establishes the Key or name of the scale at each fret.

E SCALE

E MAJOR SCALE (Moveable)

E CHORD: E G# B

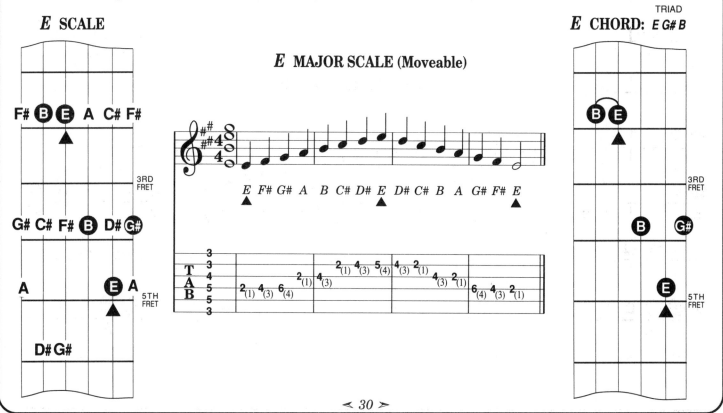

3/9/96

SCALE PATTERN DEVELOPMENT

THE "C A G E D" SEQUENCE
OF CHORD/SCALE PATTERNS

ILLUSTRATION ONE

This illustration shows how the five individual
chord/scale patterns, when linked together,
covers the entire range of the fingerboard.

┌─ **PRACTICE TIP** ────────┐

To improve finger articulation, create a
simple lead line then play it in each of
the five patterns. Keep this note pattern
in the same key. *Example:* If the original
lead line (note pattern) is in the key of *C*,
play it in the *C* scale in each of the five
patterns. Vary the tempo, play quarter
notes, eighth notes and sixteenth notes.
└───────────────────────────┘

STREET SMARTS

Great players know how to connect these patterns together with linear and zig-zag movements. Try it!

< 31 >

CAGED SEQUENCE

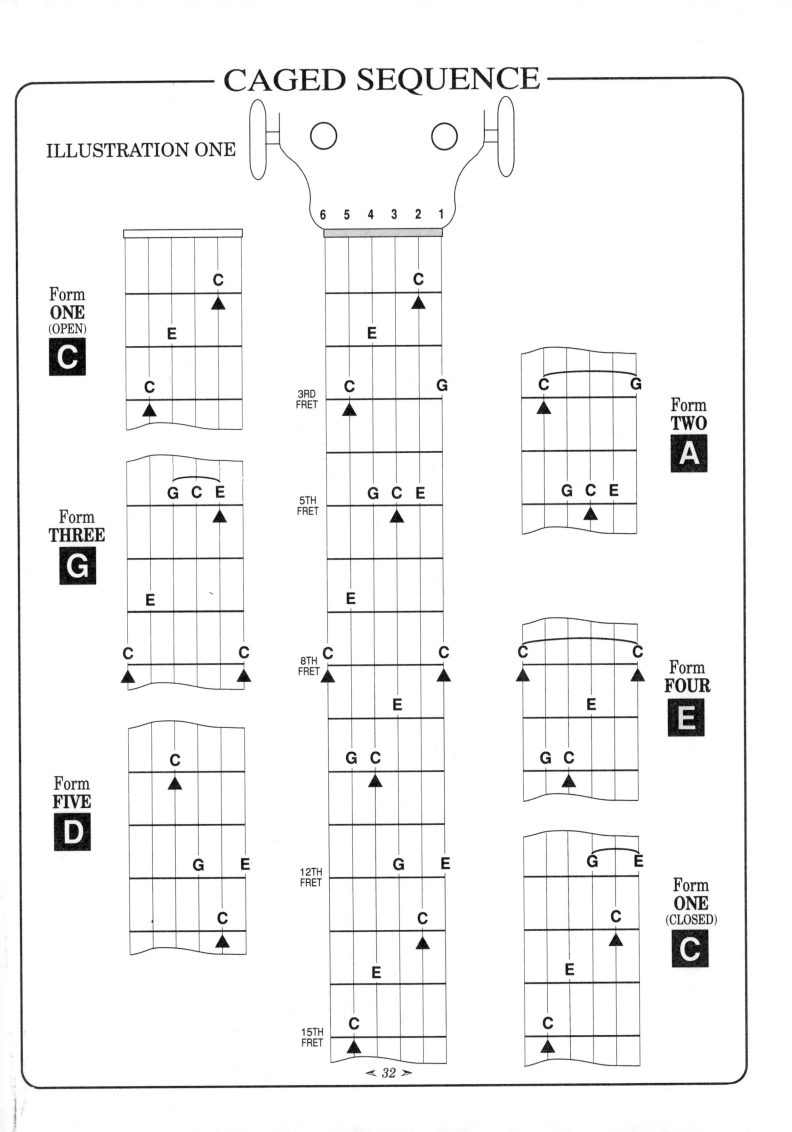

< 32 >

SCALE PATTERN DEVELOPMENT

We now begin our study of movable scale patterns. It is important to develop the ability to improvise from within each pattern, for as you will come to understand the individual finger characteristics of each pattern spurs originality. Often, "licks" played comfortable in one pattern become awkward when played in another. Also, remember that each pattern overlaps its respective chord. It is always simpler to identify a chord position than the appropriate scale position. By developing the ability to improvise effectively in all five patterns, you will never be caught wondering where the next phrase or solo should be played.

ILLUSTRATION ONE

Each scale pattern and its respective chord ascend and descend chromatically We indicate the Tonic note of the scale and chord with a black triangle so you will know which string determines its alphabetic name. Remember: Since each scale pattern moves through the entire range of the fingerboard, the mastery of one scale pattern actually provides you with the skill to play in all twelve keys. A "lick" or "solo" learned in one key may be played in all keys without any change in fingering. In effect, everything you develop through practice and experience may be multiplied by twelve!

NOTE PLACEMENT The Note Placement diagram places all notes of each pattern on the fingerboard. The shaded notes mark the octave within individual patterns.

SCALE DEGREES The Scale Degree diagram, marks each scale note by its degree number. Learn where each scale tone, by degree number, lies within each scale. Example: Where is the second degree note, the third, the fifth?

ILLUSTRATION TWO

STUDY EXERCISE
Practice each exercise and develop the finger articulation required so you may play each scale pattern with skill and ease.

PRACTICE TIP
Learn the individual sound of each scale pattern. Train yourself to sing with the guitar. Move around within the scale, skip intervals, learn to predict tones before they are played. Develop a trained ear, and the skill to play correctly any note you can sing.

STREET SMARTS
The ability to begin playing from specific notes within a major scale and the ability to hear chord harmony within the context of the scale are the keys to improvisation.

< 33 >

SCALE PATTERN DEVELOPMENT

ILLUSTRATION ONE

C PATTERN – FORM ONE

Note Placement

Scale Degrees

D MAJOR SCALE (Moveable)

D E F# G A B C# D C# B A G F# E D

ILLUSTRATION TWO   *BOSSANOVA TEMPO 132*

STUDY EXERCISE

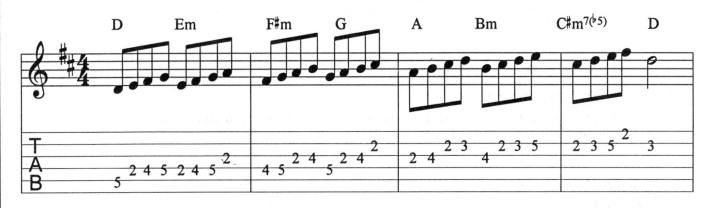

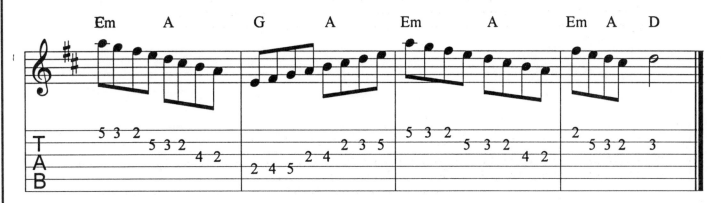

< 34 >

3/16/96

SCALE PATTERN DEVELOPMENT

ILLUSTRATION ONE

A PATTERN – FORM TWO

Note Placement

Scale Degrees

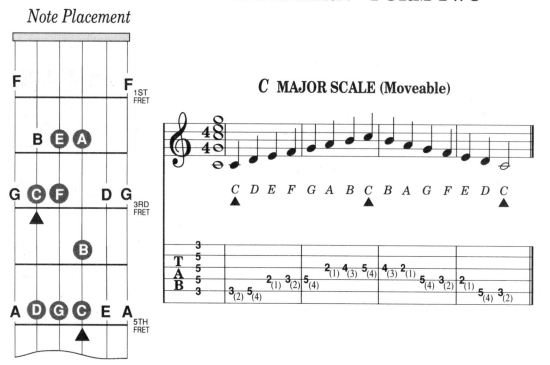

C MAJOR SCALE (Moveable)

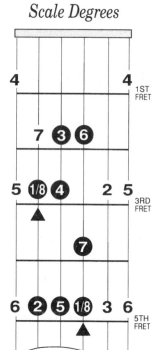

ILLUSTRATION TWO ⟨13⟩ *ROCK & ROLL TEMPO 129*

STUDY EXERCISE

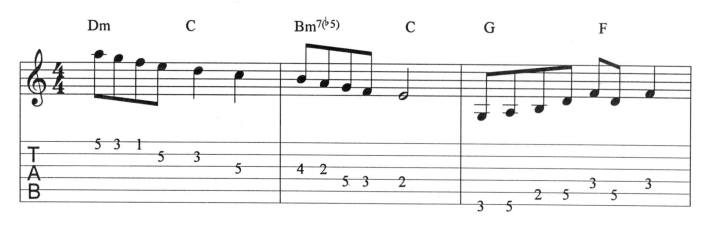

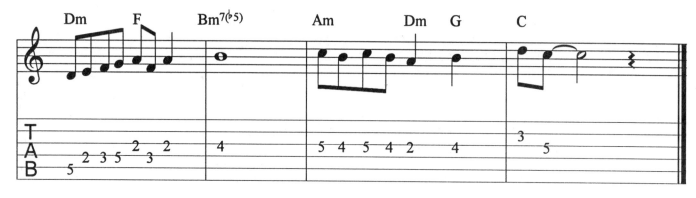

SCALE PATTERN DEVELOPMENT

ILLUSTRATION ONE

Note Placement

G PATTERN – FORM THREE

Scale Degrees

A MAJOR SCALE (Moveable)

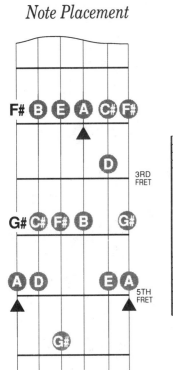

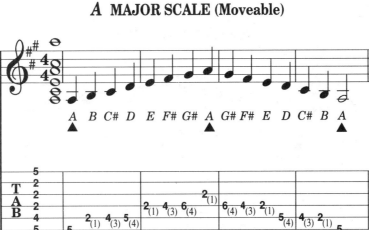

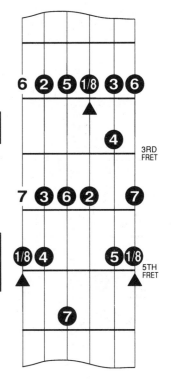

ILLUSTRATION TWO (14)

6
8 FEEL TEMPO 78

STUDY EXERCISE

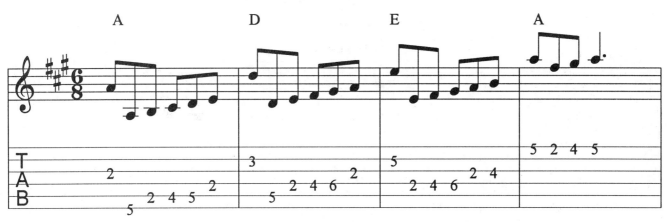

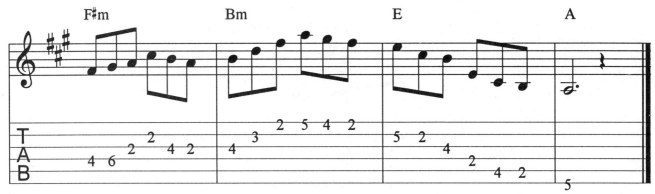

< 36 >

3/23/96

SCALE PATTERN DEVELOPMENT

ILLUSTRATION ONE

E PATTERN – FORM FOUR

Note Placement

Scale Degrees

G MAJOR SCALE (Moveable)

ILLUSTRATION TWO (15) *RAP TEMPO 113*

STUDY EXERCISE

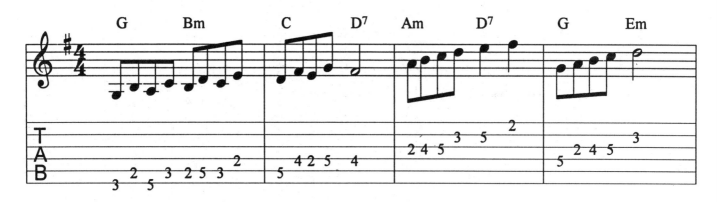

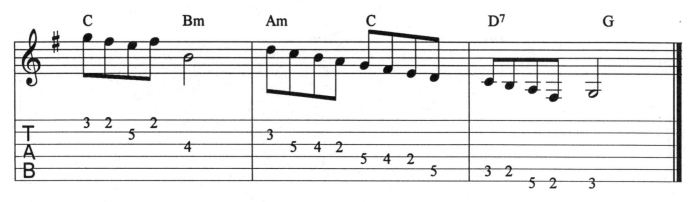

< 37 >

SCALE PATTERN DEVELOPMENT

ILLUSTRATION ONE

Note Placement

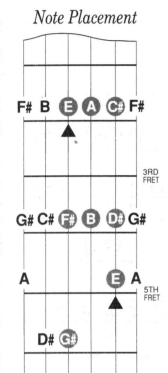

D PATTERN – FORM FIVE

E MAJOR SCALE (Moveable)

E F# G# A B C# D# E D# C# B A G# F# E

Scale Degrees

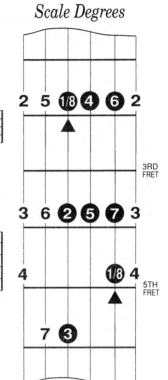

ILLUSTRATION TWO 🎧(16) COUNTRY TEMPO 111

STUDY EXERCISE

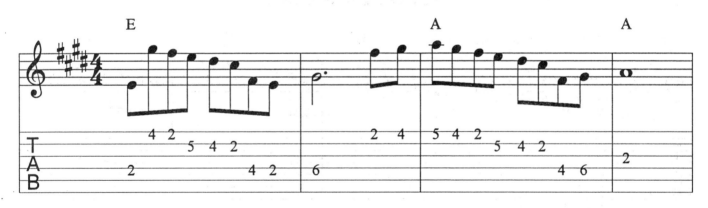

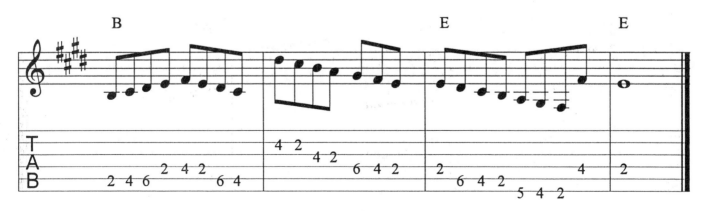

SCALE PATTERN DEVELOPMENT

section two REVIEW

STREET SMARTS

Great players know how to connect these patterns together with linear and zig-zag movments. Try it!

PAGE 31

STREET SMARTS

*By playing the **fingering pattern** correctly, you have played the **scale** correctly!*

PAGE 23

STREET SMARTS

The ability to begin playing from specific notes within a major scale and the ability to hear chord harmony within the context of the scale are one of the keys to improvisation.

PAGE 33

---

section three

CHORD HARMONY STUDY

Improvisational solos follow a few well-defined rules of chord harmony. A trained ear, knowledge of chord triads, and a developed sense of rhythmic structure constitutes the bedrock of creative music. Just playing chords will not be enough if you want to create lead lines. To solo, you must come to understand the infrastructure of chords; triads, tonality, and how progressions resolve. One of the greatest assets you can acquire in your study of improvisation is how the scale is harmonized and what chords belong to each key.

> **SUCCESS IS ASSURED TO THOSE WHO SET GOALS AND FOLLOW THROUGH WITH COMMITMENT.**
>
> *You must know what you want, then develop the desire for its attainment. Desire and hard work make up for a shortage of talent.*

─ CHORD HARMONY STUDY ─

HARMONIZING THE MAJOR SCALE

"The secret to improvisation, "how to make music", is as simple as ABC. Well almost, let's say *AC#E*, or *FAC, GBD, EG#B*. The ability to successfully play lead lines over chord progressions is as simple as knowing diatonic chord triads – the three notes that form each diatonic chord".

– Triadic Improvisation: Wilbur M. Savidge

ILLUSTRATION ONE

Composers and arrangers have simple rules to aid them in writing harmony, and to understand these rules will enable you easily determine which chords belong to each key.

The Major Scale is harmonized by creating three note chords over each degree of the scale. How is this accomplished? First, we write out a diatonic major scale. In our example we use the *C Major* Scale: *C D E F G A B C*.

ILLUSTRATION TWO

We then count up three notes, an interval of a third, and write another scale in parallel over the first scale. This is accomplished by using only notes of the original scale. The first note of the second scale is the note *E (CDE)* – a third interval. Our new scale is : *EFGABCDE*.

ILLUSTRATION THREE

To complete our three note chord, we again count up a third interval – *(EFG)*, and write another parallel scale using only the original scale notes. Our third scale: *GABCDEFG*.

The major scale contains seven different notes and we now have created seven different three note triads called chords. Because each chord contains only notes from the original scale, they are said to be diatonic to the key of *C* , (Diatonic Harmony).

ILLUSTRATION FOUR

DIATONIC SEVENTH CHORD

In our study, "Harmonizing The Major Scale", we explained how the chord triad is created by stacking notes in intervals of a third. The triad (three notes) produces major and minor chords. If we continue stacking "thirds" to extend each chords tonality, it is possible to harmonize the scale with four note chords. A four note chord, stacking four third intervals, creates SEVENTH chords. Each chord contains only notes of the parent scale and is said to be diatonic to the key of which the scale is written. This sequence of chords is known as DIATONIC SEVENTH CHORDS.

── *STREET SMARTS* ──

Scales, harmonized with triads, is the basic principle upon which all harmony is built. It is this concept that sets this book apart from all books you may study. Memorize chord triads and become familiar with the three notes that form each chord in all keys. A little further on in this book, we will reveal a startling improvisational concept based on chord triads!

< 41 >

HARMONIZING THE MAJOR SCALE

ILLUSTRATION ONE (17)

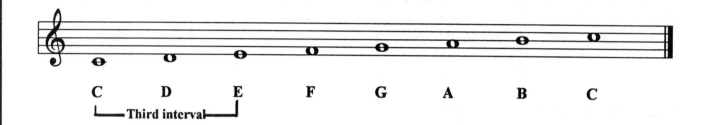

| C | D | E | F | G | A | B | C |

└─ Third interval ─┘

ILLUSTRATION TWO

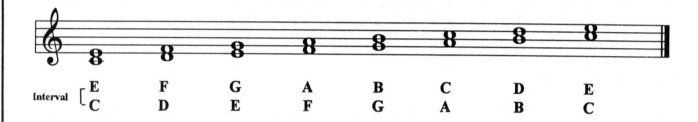

Interval
| E | F | G | A | B | C | D | E |
| C | D | E | F | G | A | B | C |

ILLUSTRATION THREE

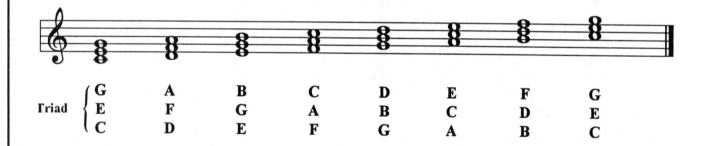

Triad
G	A	B	C	D	E	F	G
E	F	G	A	B	C	D	E
C	D	E	F	G	A	B	C

ILLUSTRATION FOUR

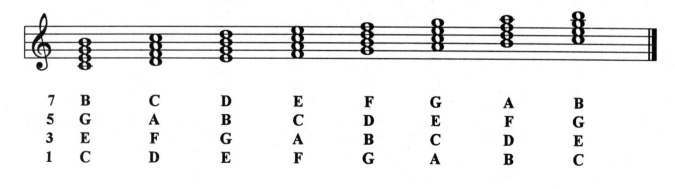

7	B	C	D	E	F	G	A	B
5	G	A	B	C	D	E	F	G
3	E	F	G	A	B	C	D	E
1	C	D	E	F	G	A	B	C

CHORD HARMONY STUDY

RELATIONSHIP OF CHORDS

ILLUSTRATION ONE

The scale harmonized in thirds establishes the type of chord created at each degree of a Major scale. Chords built on the first, fourth, and fifth degrees are Major type chords. Chords built on the second, third and sixth degrees are Minor chords. The chord built on the Seventh degree is called a Minor flat five chord (a minor chord with a flatted fifth).

CHORD SEQUENCE:

(1) Major, (2) Minor, (3) Minor, (4) Major, (5) Major, (6) Minor, (7) Minor flat five.

The chords formed by harmonizing the C Major scale in thirds are: *C, Dmi, Emi, F, G, Ami, Bmib5*. Extended "color tone" chords are: *Cmaj7, Dm7, Em7, F Maj7, G7, Am7, Bm7b5*.

RULES OF CHORD HARMONY

ILLUSTRATION TWO

The chords formed by harmonizing the diatonic scale in thirds are organized into two groups: primary chords, and secondary chords. Chords built on the Tonic (1), the Sub Dominant (4), and the Dominant (5), create a natural progression of major sounds (as opposed to minor sounds), and are called the Primary Chords. Chords built on the second, third, sixth, and the seventh degree are minor chords called Secondary Chords.

TONIC (1) chord may resolve to any chord.

SUPER TONIC (2) chord may resolve to any chord except the Tonic (1).

MEDIANT (3) chord may resolve to any chord except the Tonic (1), or Dominant (5) chord.

SUB-DOMINANT (4) chord may resolve to any chord.

DOMINANT (5) chord may resolve to any chord except the Super Tonic (2), or the Leading Tone (7).

SUB-MEDIANT (6) chord may resolve to any chord except the Tonic (1), or the Leading Tone (7).

LEADING TONE (7) chord may resolve to any chord except the Super Tonic (2), or the Sub-Dominant (4).

< 43 >

RELATIONSHIP OF CHORDS

ILLUSTRATION ONE

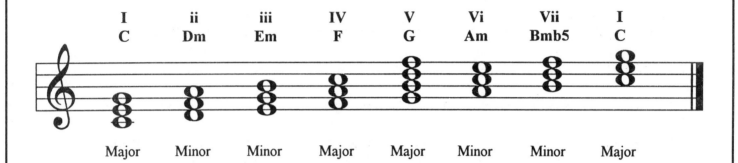

RULES OF CHORD HARMONY

ILLUSTRATION TWO

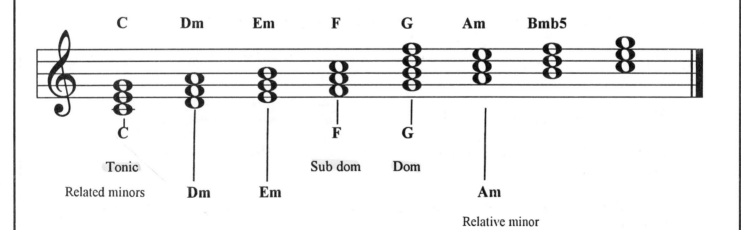

< 44 >

CHORD HARMONY STUDY

PRIMARY CHORDS

The key signature establishes the key in which a piece is written. Scales, chords, melody, and harmony must confirm to the tonality set by the key signature. This inter-relationship between the scale and the chords, created by harmonizing the scale in third intervals, produces tonality the way sentences work together to produce a paragraph.

Not all, but most chord progressions center around the three primary chords: the Tonic (1), Sub-dominant (1V), and Dominant (V), a sequence of chords that establishes the Key Center or the tonality of the scale. This phenomenon occurs because of the interaction of active and inactive tones within each chord.

The Tonic chord is inactive, at rest. The Sub Dominant and Dominant chords are active and demand resolution. The Dominant chord (V) is most active when played as a Dominant Seventh chord (*G7, A7 C7* etc.). Why? Because it is formed by adding a minor third interval over the basic triad. This produces a flat seventh: a tone that is non- diatonic to the scale established by the Key Signature. The addition of this one non-diatonic tone creates a tonality that demands resolution back to the Tonic which is the point of rest.

While there are various ways to play chord progressions, chords eventually reach the Dominant Seventh (V7) and from there resolve to the Tonic (1) chord.

TONIC CHORD

The first and eight degree of the scale is called the TONIC. It is the point against which all other values are measured. From the Tonic, chords progress through a series of sounds that adds tension and color. Progressions normally begin and end on the Tonic. Why? Because it is the home chord, or the prominent point of rest.

SUB DOMINANT

The forth degree of the scale (1V) is called the Sub Dominant. It is closely related to the Tonic and its appearance establishes a strong gravitational movement toward the Tonic chord. The Sub Dominant chord may also move to the Dominant chord.

DOMINANT CHORD

The Dominant Seventh chord (V7) is of special importance in improvisation, not only because of the prominence of Dominant harmony, but also because the Dominate Seventh has properties not shared by other chords. The Dominant Seventh is built with a TRITONE interval, three whole steps, between the third and seventh degrees. This creates a dissonance which is responsible for the chords active sound and strong gravitational movement toward the Tonic (1).

SECONDARY CHORDS

SUPER TONIC (ii), MEDIANT (iii), and the SUB-MEDIANT (Vi), are minor chords. Minor chords are constructed by combining a Minor 3rd interval with a Major 3rd. This lowers the minor chord"s third one semi-tone, which creates the chords minor tonality. The Super Tonic,(ii) chord can be used in substitution of the 1V chord. Secondary chords are used also as transitional chords to effect a movement to and from major chords.

< 45 >

CHORD HARMONY STUDY

EXTENDED DOMINANT SEVENTH CHORDS
COLOR TONES

During the early Jazz era, musician searching for ways to add interest and color to harmony chords, began to extend the basic chord triad by including the 9th, 11th and 13th scale tones. The Dominant Seventh, because of its strong tonal movement, was the ideal chord with which to explore this new concept in chordal harmony. Today, musicians still make frequent use of extended Dominant Seventh chords. (*Example: C9, A11, G13*).

It must be noted that it is the 3rd and 7th tone which define the quality of the chord, and are the most important color tones. The lowered 3rd makes a minor chord, the lowered 7th creates the Dominant Seventh. The 5th of the dominant chord is often dropped because of the fingering limitation imposed by the guitar.

The usage of 9ths, 11ths and 13ths are considered extended "color" tones. They are optional and may be included, or omitted, in any combination. The extended color tone has no effect on the way the dominant chord functions in chord harmony, and extended chords are used freely as substitution for the dominant seventh chord.

ILLUSTRATION ONE   Key of *G* Major

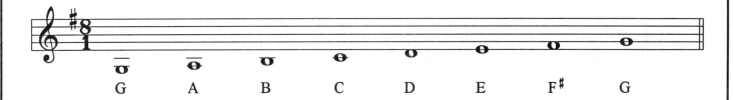

8	9	10	11	12	13		
1	2	3	4	5	6	7	8
G	A	B	C	D	E	F#	G

ILLUSTRATION TWO   EXTENDED
DOMINANT SEVENTH CHORDS
(Moveable Chord Forms)

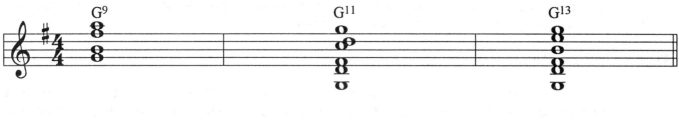

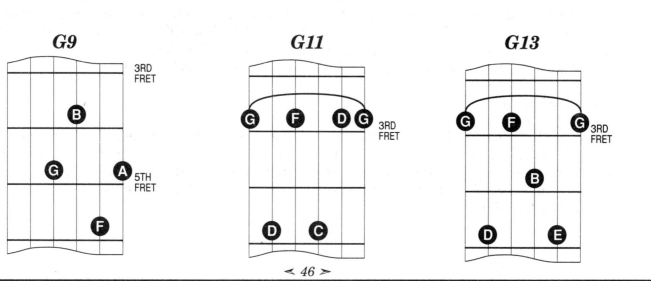

G9   *G11*   *G13*

< 46 >

CHORD HARMONY STUDY

DOMINANT SEVENTH CHORDS
AND THE
MIXOLYDIAN SCALE

ILLUSTRATION ONE

The triad of the dominant seventh chord, built from the notes of the chords scale, will because of the dominant chords lowered seventh, share in common the notes of the scale in which the song is written. (Key Signature Scale.) Example: Key of *C Major* – Notes: *CDEFGABC*. The dominant seventh chord (5th degree) is *G7*. The parent scale of the G7 chord is *G Major*: *GABCDEF#G*. The formula for building a dominant seventh chord 1 3 5 ♭7, creates a *G7* chord comprised of *GBDF*, notes of the *C Major* Scale.

ILLUSTRATION TWO

The Mixolydian Scale places the half-steps between the 3-4 degrees and the 6-7 degrees. This placement of the half-steps produces a scale that may be played over dominant seventh chords of the same letter name.

PRACTICE TIP

Strum the *G7* chord. Then, play the *C* scale, commencing on the 5th degree, the note *G*, and play through the scale stopping on the octave note *G*.

STREET SMARTS

*The Mixolydian Scale **is** the scale of choice to play over dominant seventh chords.*

< 47 >

CHORD HARMONY STUDY

DOMINANT SEVENTH CHORDS
AND THE MIXOLYDIAN MODE

ILLUSTRATION ONE

Key of *C* Major

1	2	3	4	5	6	7	8
C	D	E	F	G	A	B	C

Key of *G* Major

1	2	3	4	5	6	♭7	7	8	
G	A	B	C	D	E	7	F#	G	
G		B		D		7			*TRIAD NOTES*
1		3		5		♭7			

ILLUSTRATION TWO

G Mixolydian Mode

1	2	3	4	5	6	7	8
G	A	B	C	D	E	F	G

< 48 >

3/30/96

CHORD HARMONY STUDY
ARPEGGIOS

Arpeggios are some or all notes of a chord played one at a time. There are Major, Minor, Diminished and Augmented arpeggios. We will study the Major and Minor. Arpeggios provide the guitarist with a unique way to add variety and new sounds to established scale "licks", for arpeggios are a bridge between scales and chords. Also, playing across a chord covers the strings more quickly than playing a scale run. The basic arpeggio is created by playing the chord triad one note at a time or the 1-3-5 notes of the scale that form the chord.

Skipping across strings at random will create unique sounds not possible when playing a scale. Arpeggios may be played in ascending or descending order.

FORM ONE *C* SCALE PATTERN   (Key of *D* Major)

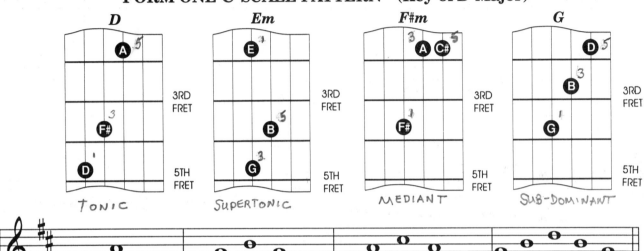

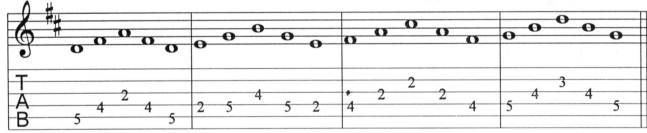

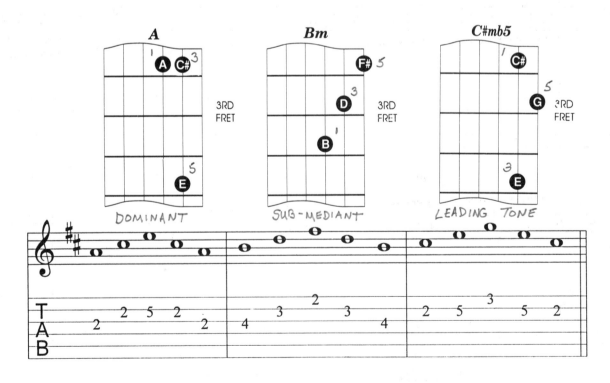

< 49 >

CHORD HARMONY STUDY

C PATTERN ARPEGGIOS

EXAMPLE: 18

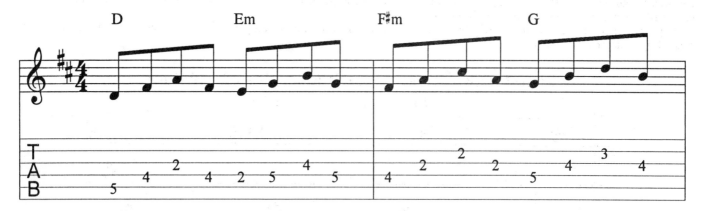

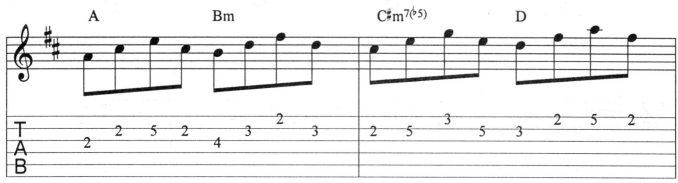

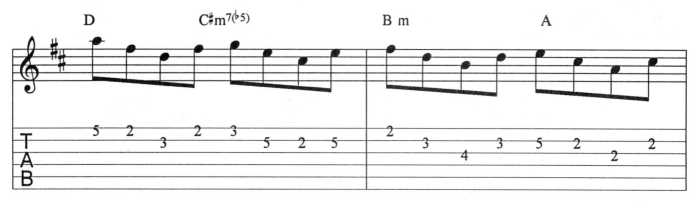

PRACTICE TIP

1. Play the arpeggio, then stum the chord it relates to.
2. Practice this example in the other four patterns and forms.

4/6/96

CHORD HARMONY STUDY

ARPEGGIOS

FORM TWO *A* SCALE PATTERN (Key of *C*)

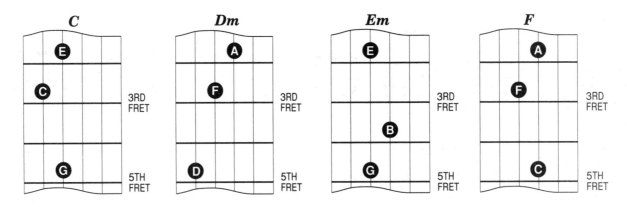

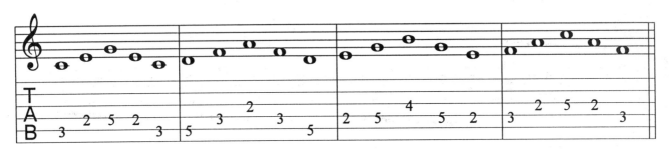

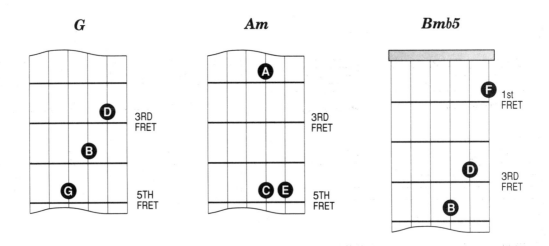

< 51 >

CHORD HARMONY STUDY

A PATTERN ARPEGGIOS

EXAMPLE: 19

< 52 >

4/13/96

ARPEGGIOS

FORM THREE *G* SCALE PATTERN (Key of *A*)

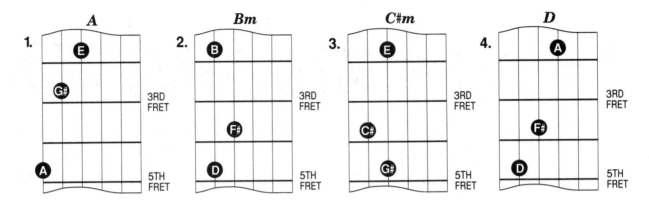

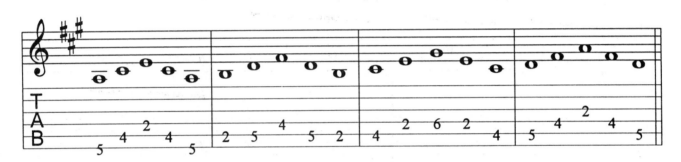

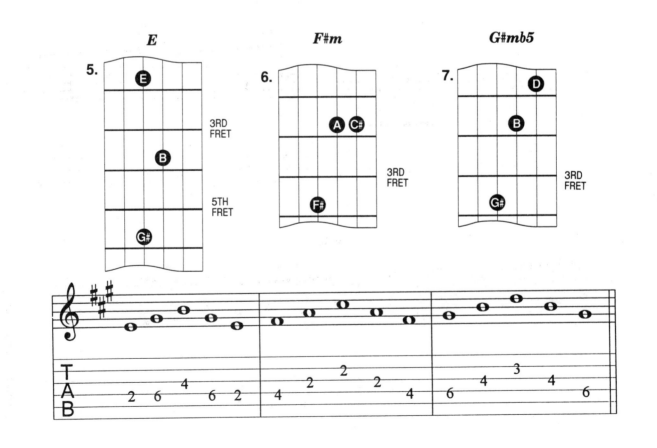

< 53 >

G PATTERN ARPEGGIOS (Key of *A*)

EXAMPLE: 20

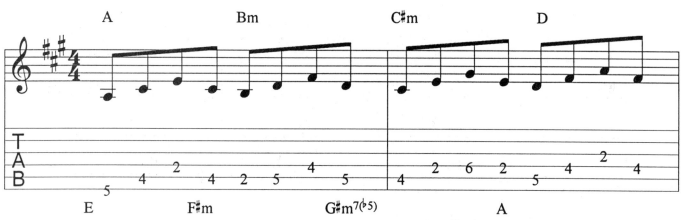

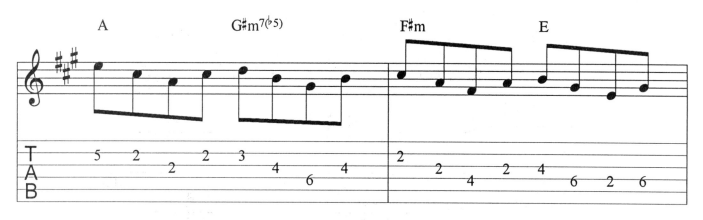

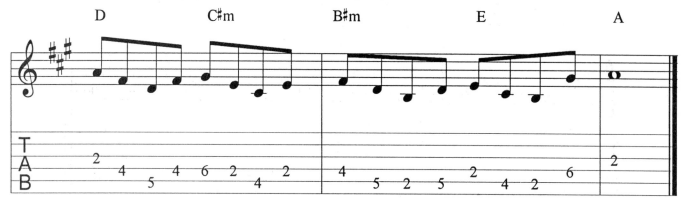

CHORD HARMONY STUDY

ARPEGGIOS

FORM FOUR *E* SCALE PATTERN   (Key of *G*)

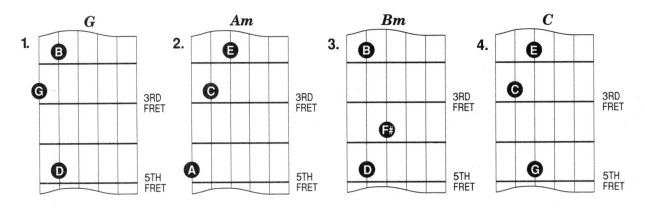

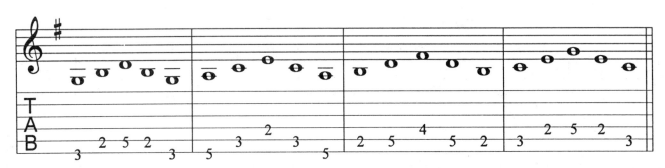

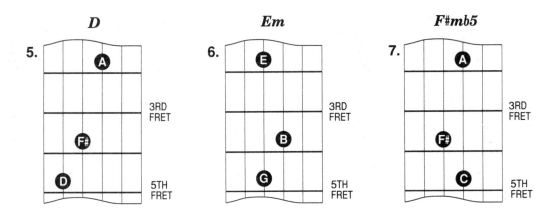

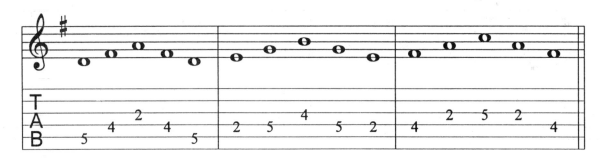

< 55 >

CHORD HARMONY STUDY

E PATTERN ARPEGGIOS (Key of *G*)
EXAMPLE: 21

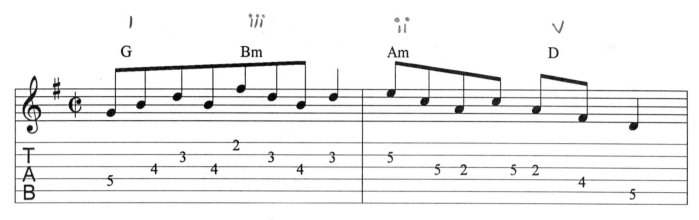

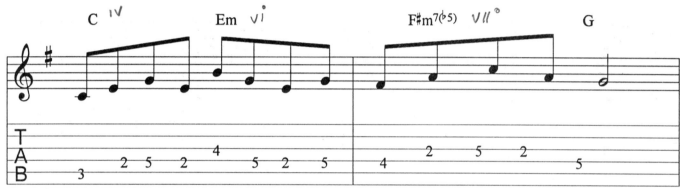

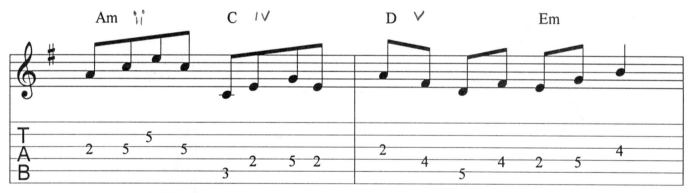

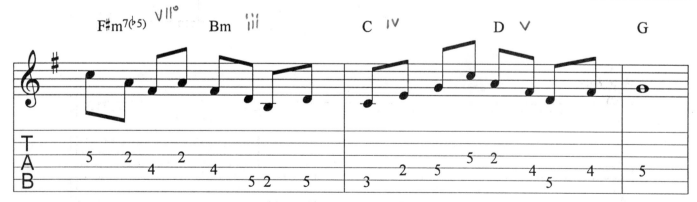

< 56 >

CHORD HARMONY STUDY

ARPEGGIOS

FORM FIVE *D* SCALE PATTERN   (Key of *E*)

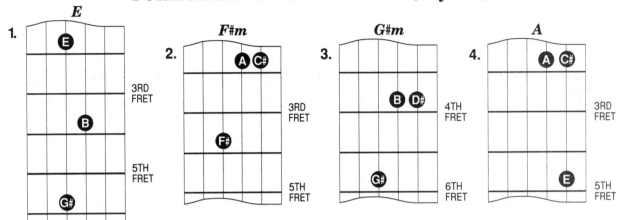

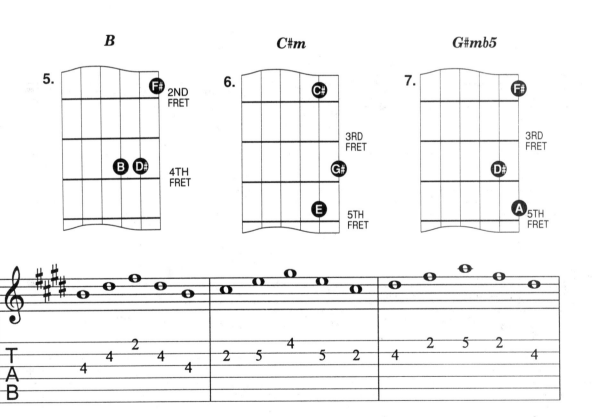

< 57 >

CHORD HARMONY STUDY

D PATTERN ARPEGGIOS (Key of *E*)

EXAMPLE: 22

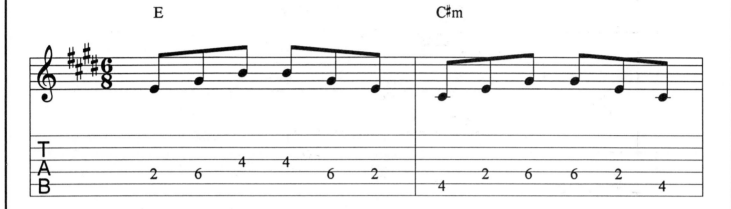

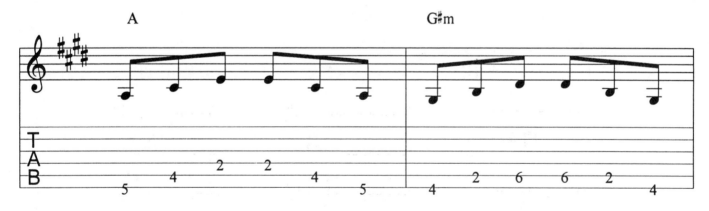

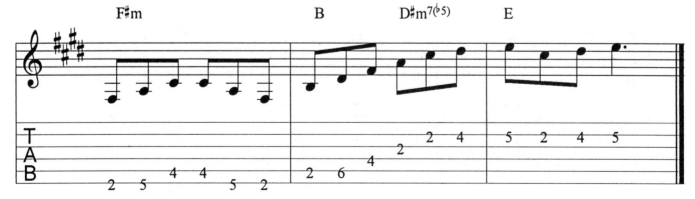

< 58 >

SCALE PATTERN DEVELOPMENT

section three REVIEW

STREET SMARTS

Scales, harmonized with triads, is the basic principle upon which all harmony is built. It is this concept that sets this book apart from all books you may study. Memorize chord triads and become familiar with the three notes that form each chord in all keys. A little further on in this book, we will reveal a startling improvisational concept based on chord triads!

PAGE 41

STREET SMARTS

*The Mixolydian Scale **is** the scale of choice to play over the dominant seventh chord.*

PAGE 47

STREET SMARTS

Practice arpeggio playing because the three notes that form the chord (the triad) function as guide tones (starting notes) from which we may start our solos.

PAGE 49

< 59 >

MODAL PLAYING

Music can be quite confusing and books offer little insight into the creative aspect of music. What must you know, what is the secret the great players have come to understand? In this section of "Scales Over Chords", we present the one element of music all great guitarists have learned – how to use modes to create exciting and original lead lines and "licks". Master this section and you are well on your way to being the guitarist you desire to be.

> **SURMOUNTING DIFFFICULTIES IS A STATE OF MIND.**
>
> *If you believe strongly enough in your desires, you will most certainly obtain them.*

< 60 >

MODAL PLAYING

MODES
THE SCALES OF IMPROVISATION

There is a basic relationship between chords in any given major key and the scales that may be played. To improvise effectively, you must know which scale goes with each chord. Remember: We are teaching you to play, Scales Over Chords!

While the Major scale establishes the key and the chord group (harmony), it does impose limitations when improvising lead lines. As a result, musicians often use modal scales in order to add originality, color, and interest to their solos.

ILLUSTRATION ONE

MODAL TERMINOLOGY
Modes represent an alternative to the melodic and harmonic structure of the diatonic scale. Diatonic scales and modes have different applications. The diatonic scale determines harmony (chords) while modes express melodic variations. The Dorian, Phrygian, and Aeolian modes create minor sounds, the Ionian, Lydian, and Mixolydian modes create major sounds, and the Locrian, a diminished sound. The overall mood of each mode can be heard by playing chords build on the first note of each mode.

A MODE is a series of eight notes played within the structure of the diatonic scale, the parent scale. A Major scale begins on the first degree, the Tonic note, and this is also called the IONIAN mode; a scale played from the first degree. Simply speaking, modes are scales created by starting on any of the seven notes of the diatonic scale.

ILLUSTRATION ONE

The Major scale is a set arrangement of intervals that places the half-steps between the third-fourth degrees, and the seventh-eight degrees. This pattern is altered by starting a scale on any degree other then One (tonic). Example: a DORIAN mode is a scale played from the second degree which places the half steps between the second-third, and the sixth-seventh degrees, this altered major scale creates a minor sound.

ILLUSTRATION TWO

THE MODAL SYSTEM

(1) The IONIAN mode is created by playing a diatonic scale from the first degree to the octave note.

(2) The DORIAN mode is created by playing a diatonic scale from the second degree to the octave note.

(3) The PHRYGIAN mode is created by playing a diatonic scale from the third degree to the octave note.

(4) The LYDIAN mode is created by playing a diatonic scale from the fourth degree to the octave note.

(5) The MIXOLYDIAN mode is created by playing a diatonic scale from the fifth degree to the octave note.

(6) The AEOLIAN mode is created by playing a diatonic scale from the sixth degree to the octave note.

(7) The LOCRIAN mode is created by playing a diatonic scale from the seventh degree to the octave note.

STREET SMARTS
Modal improvisation is as simple as playing a diatonic scale!

< 61 >

INTRODUCTION TO MODES

MODAL TERMINOLOGY
C MAJOR

ILLUSTRATION ONE

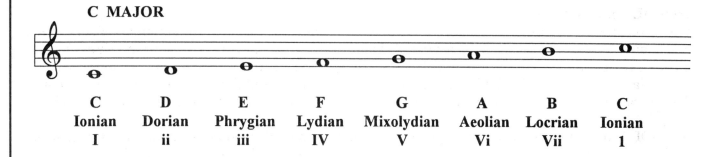

C MAJOR

C	D	E	F	G	A	B	C
Ionian	Dorian	Phrygian	Lydian	Mixolydian	Aeolian	Locrian	Ionian
I	ii	iii	IV	V	Vi	Vii	1

ILLUSTRATION TWO

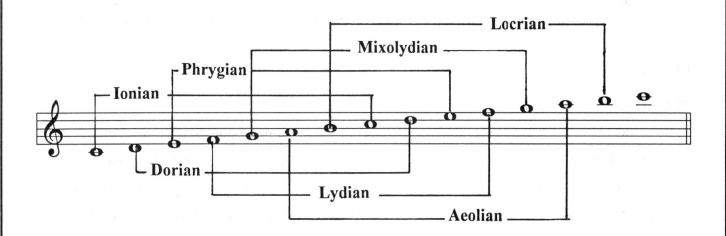

< 62 >

MODAL PLAYING

DERIVATIVE MODES
Modes derived from the Major Scale

A MODE is an INVERSION of a Major Scale, a variation created by starting on any note other then the Tonic (1). Each new scale created displaces the step, half step pattern that produces diatonic harmony. Each mode covers the range of a chromatic scale, and like the Diatonic Major Scale, steps through the thirteen-note octave. However, the step, half-step pattern particular to each mode produces a different series of scale tones. This new pattern causes dissonance which creates the individual characteristics of each mode.

When a mode is built upon a note of the parent scale, we call it a derivative to modal construction. When a mode is built from its Tonic note, utilizing the correct modal step, half-step pattern, we call it a parallel approach.

We will use the derivative approach in our study of modes. Derivative scales actually create only five modes since the Ionian mode is the Major scale (same step, half-step pattern) and the Aeolian mode is the Natural Minor Scale.

The Ionian (*I-O-NE-AN*) Mode

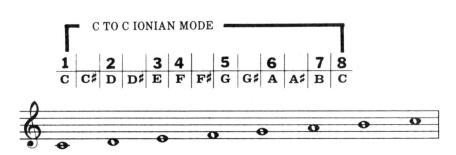

The Dorian (*DOR-E-AN*) Mode

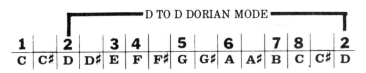

The Phrygian (*FRIG-E-AN*) Mode

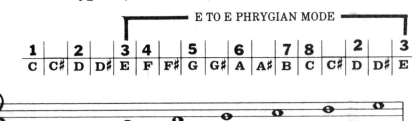

< 63 >

DERIVATIVE MODES

The Lydian (*LID-E-AN*) Mode

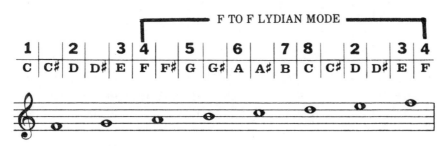

The Mixolydian (*MIX-O-LID-E-AN*) Mode

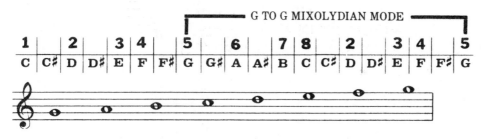

The Aeolian (*E-O-LE-AN*) Mode

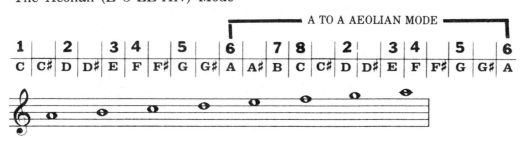

The Locrian (*LO-CRI-AN*) Mode

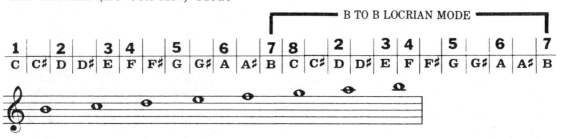

MODES DERIVED FROM MAJOR SCALES

A derivative mode is created by beginning a new scale on a degree of the parent scale and using only the notes of the parent scale. A derivative mode is played in parallel to the parent scale.

ILLUSTRATION ONE

In Illustration One, we indicate the modal notes as placed within the parent major scale. The gray triangles marks the parent scale's Tonic notes. The black triangles mark the Tonic notes of the modal scale.

We have written out each major scale and the Tonic chord of that scale. Below the Major Scale, we have written out the appropriate mode. Each mode is identified by its scale degree. We also show the chord created by harmonizing the mode (1-3-5). We suggest strumming the chord, then play the mode, this will help establish the tonal identity of the mode and how it relates to the chord.

ILLUSTRATION TWO

Practice each exercise, for in each we provide you with valuable knowledge of scales and modes. Each exercise will help you achieve the finger articulation required to play well, and offers you the opportunity to develop your musical ear, the ability to hear the tonal characteristic of each mode.

PRACTICE TIP

Strum the chord, then play through the scale – then, strum the chord again. Listen to the harmony created. Create little note patterns (runs), then strum the chord. Start and stop on different notes, but always end a phrase on the parent scale's Tonic note (1) – which is of course, also the root note of the chord.

STREET SMARTS

Traditional modal studies require you to memorize scale formulas (step/half-step patterns), and over the chord each mode may be played. This is boring and confusing to novice players. We ask you to learn the notes that form the chords you commonly use, or better yet, learn how to instinctively count, in thirds, and determine triads in your head.

< 65 >

MODES DERIVED FROM MAJOR SCALES

ILLUSTRATION ONE

DORIAN MODE

Second Degree

Form One
C Scale Pattern

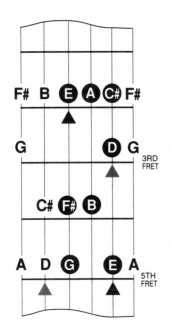

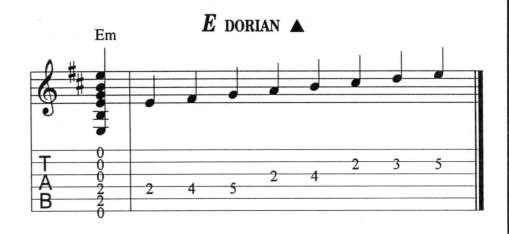

D MAJOR SCALE ▲

DORIAN

E DORIAN ▲

ILLUSTRATION TWO

 BOSSANOVA TEMPO 105

STUDY EXERCISE

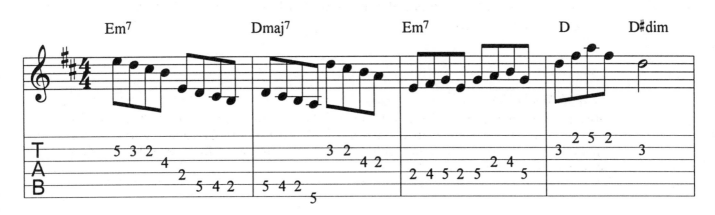

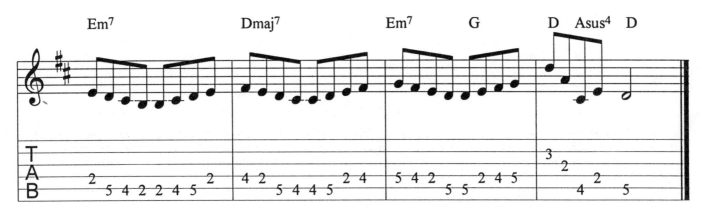

MODES DERIVED FROM MAJOR SCALES

ILLUSTRATION ONE

PHRYGIAN MODE
Third Degree

Form One
C Scale Pattern

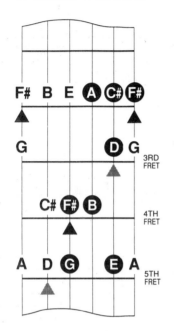

ILLUSTRATION TWO ㉕ *OLDIES BEAT TEMPO 135*

STUDY EXERCISE

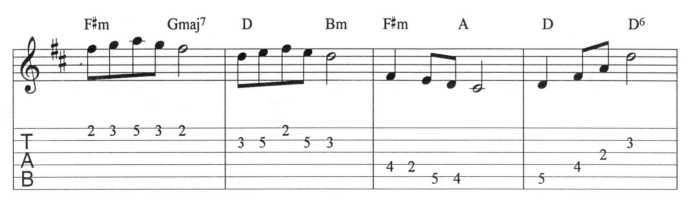

< 67 >

MODES DERIVED FROM MAJOR SCALES

ILLUSTRATION ONE

LYDIAN MODE
Fourth Degree

Form One
C Scale Pattern

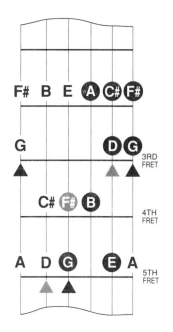

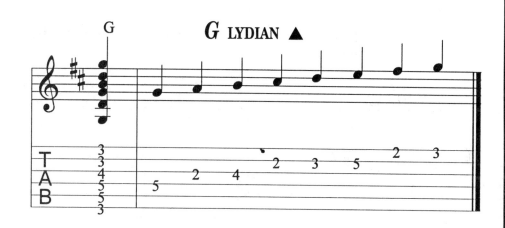

ILLUSTRATION TWO (26) *ROCK BEAT TEMPO 135*

STUDY EXERCISE

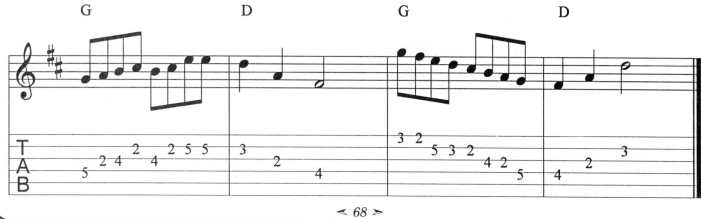

< 68 >

MODES DERIVED FROM MAJOR SCALES

ILLUSTRATION ONE

MIXOLYDIAN MODE
Fifth Degree

Form One
C Scale Pattern

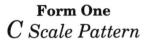

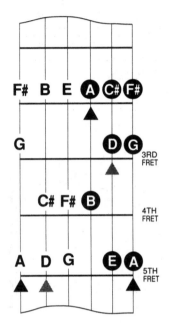

ILLUSTRATION TWO (27) *COUNTRY BEAT TEMPO 119*

STUDY EXERCISE

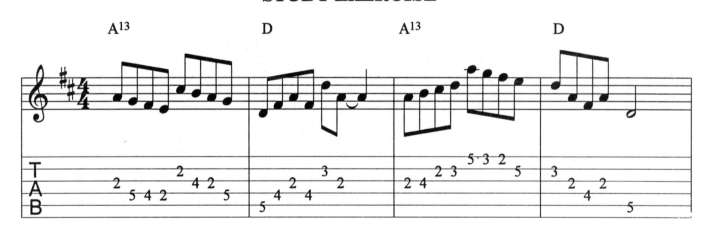

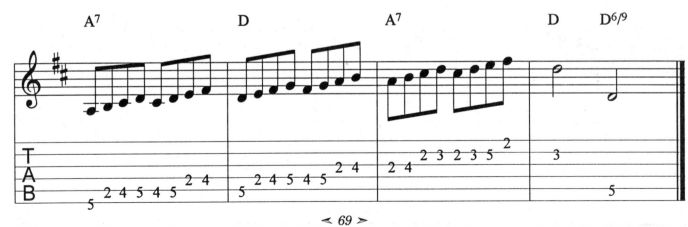

< 69 >

MODES DERIVED FROM MAJOR SCALES

ILLUSTRATION ONE

AEOLIAN MODE
Sixth Degree

Form One
C Scale Pattern

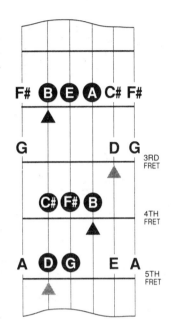

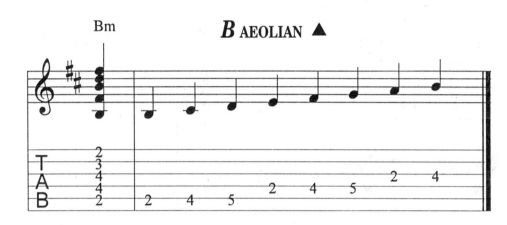

ILLUSTRATION TWO   (28)   *RAP BEAT TEMPO 94*

STUDY EXERCISE

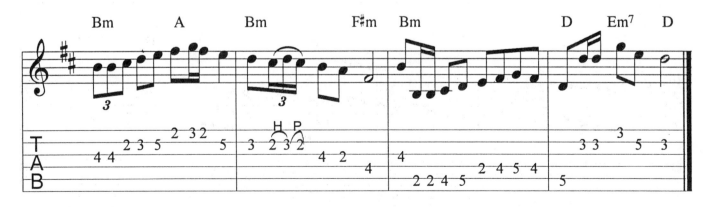

MODES DERIVED FROM MAJOR SCALES

ILLUSTRATION ONE

LOCRIAN MODE
Seventh Degree

Form One
C Scale Pattern

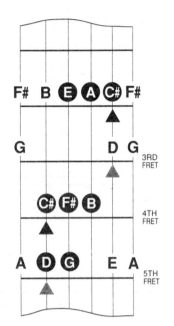

D MAJOR SCALE ▲

LOCRAIN

C# LOCRIAN ▲

ILLUSTRATION TWO (29) *6/8 BEAT TEMPO 68*

STUDY EXERCISE

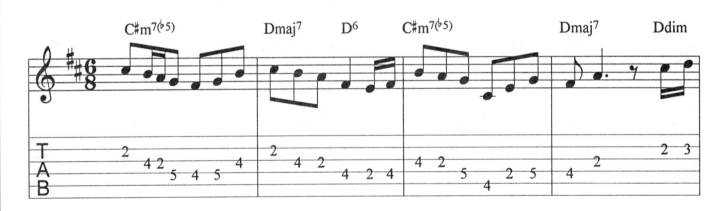

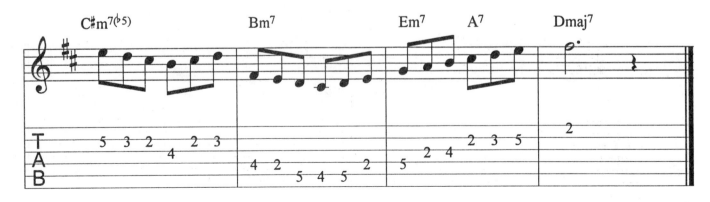

< 71 >

MODES DERIVED FROM MAJOR SCALES

ILLUSTRATION ONE

Form Two
A Scale Pattern

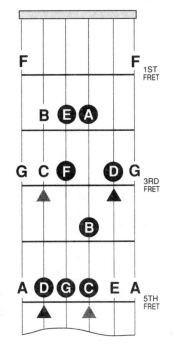

DORIAN MODE
Second Degree

C MAJOR SCALE ▲

D DORIAN ▲

ILLUSTRATION TWO (30) *ROCK BEAT TEMPO 130*

STUDY EXERCISE

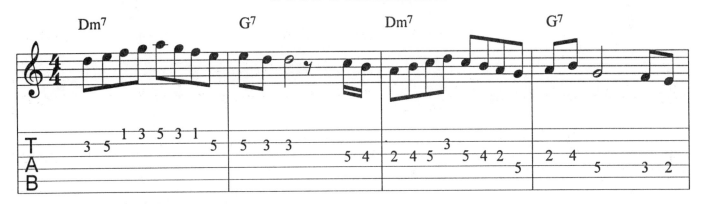

MODES DERIVED FROM MAJOR SCALES

ILLUSTRATION ONE

Form Two
A Scale Pattern

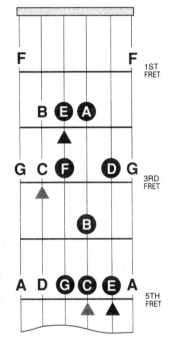

PHRYGIAN MODE
Third Degree

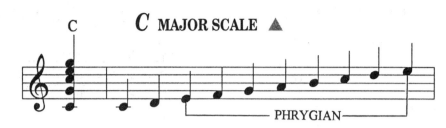

ILLUSTRATION TWO   (31)   *16 BEAT FEEL TEMPO 118*

STUDY EXERCISE

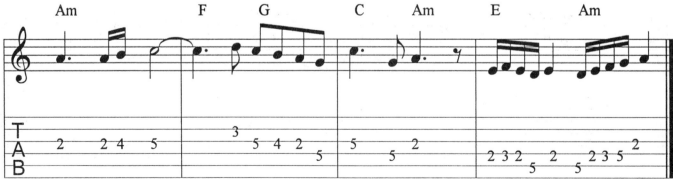

< 73 >

MODES DERIVED FROM MAJOR SCALES

ILLUSTRATION ONE

Form Two
A Scale Pattern

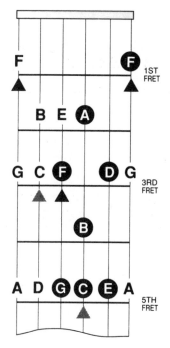

LYDIAN MODE
Fourth Degree

C MAJOR SCALE ▲

LYDIAN

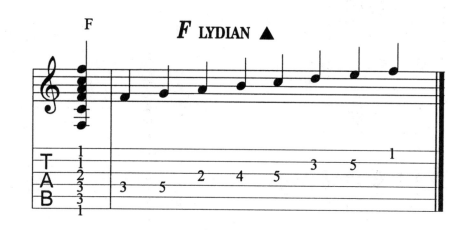

F LYDIAN ▲

ILLUSTRATION TWO

HARD ROCK TEMPO 122

STUDY EXERCISE

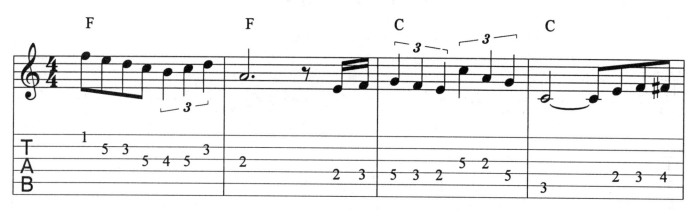

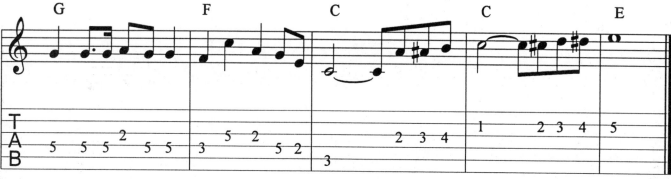

< 74 >

MODES DERIVED FROM MAJOR SCALES

ILLUSTRATION ONE

Form Two
A Scale Pattern

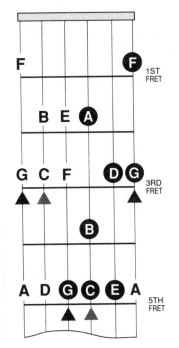

MIXOLYDIAN MODE
Fifth Degree

C MAJOR SCALE ▲

MIXOLYDIAN

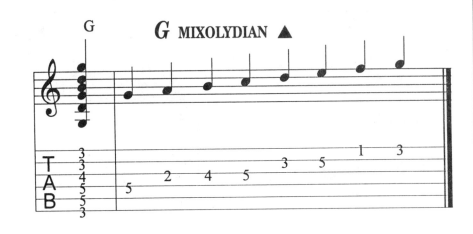

G MIXOLYDIAN ▲

ILLUSTRATION TWO

OLDIES BEAT TEMPO 178

STUDY EXERCISE

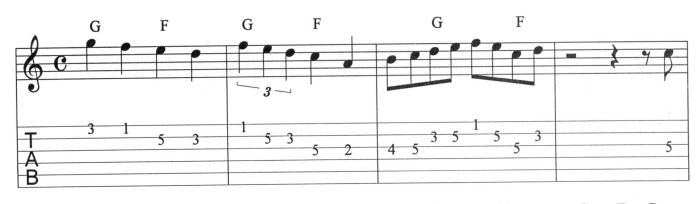

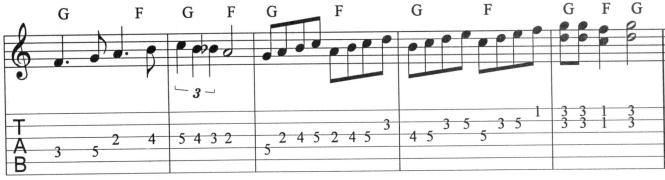

MODES DERIVED FROM MAJOR SCALES

ILLUSTRATION ONE

Form Two
A Scale Pattern

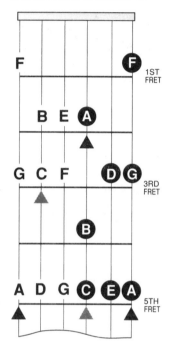

AEOLIAN MODE
Sixth Degree

C MAJOR SCALE ▲

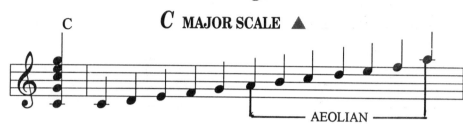

AEOLIAN

A AEOLIAN ▲

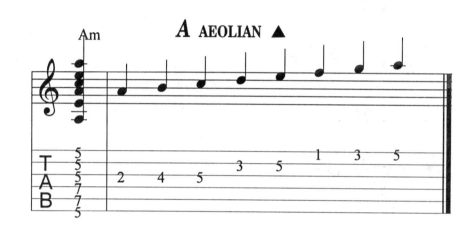

ILLUSTRATION TWO (34) *BRUSH SWING TEMPO 122*

STUDY EXERCISE

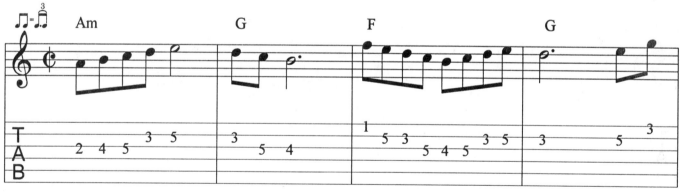

< 76 >

MODES DERIVED FROM MAJOR SCALES

ILLUSTRATION ONE

Form Two
A Scale Pattern

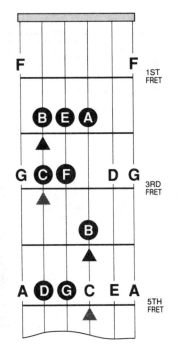

LOCRIAN MODE
Seventh Degree

C MAJOR SCALE ▲

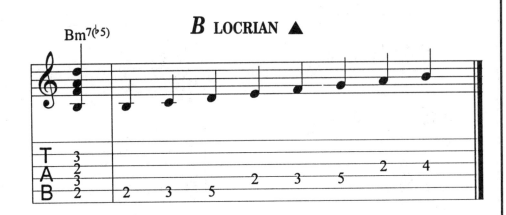

LOCRIAN

B LOCRIAN ▲

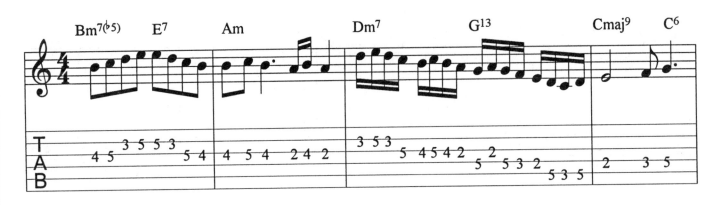

Bm⁷⁽♭⁵⁾

ILLUSTRATION TWO ㉟ LAMBADA TEMPO 126

STUDY EXERCISE

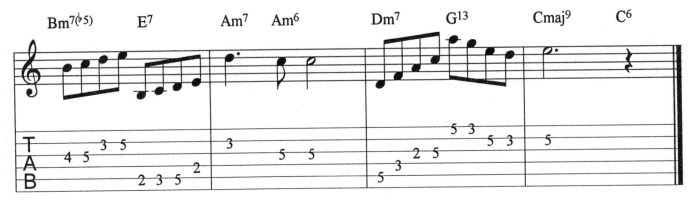

< 77 >

MODES DERIVED FROM MAJOR SCALES

ILLUSTRATION ONE

Form Three
G Scale Pattern

DORIAN MODE
Second Degree

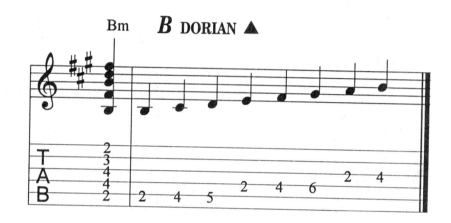

ILLUSTRATION TWO

🎧 *RHYTHM & BLUES TEMPO 110*

STUDY EXERCISE

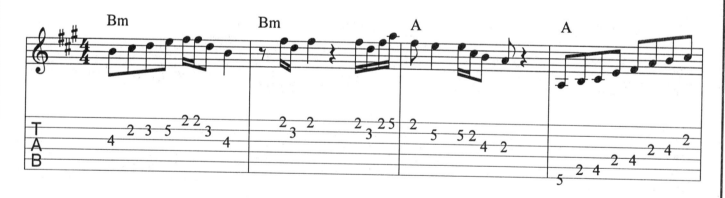

< 78 >

MODES DERIVED FROM MAJOR SCALES

ILLUSTRATION ONE

Form Three
G Scale Pattern

PHRYGIAN MODE
Third Degree

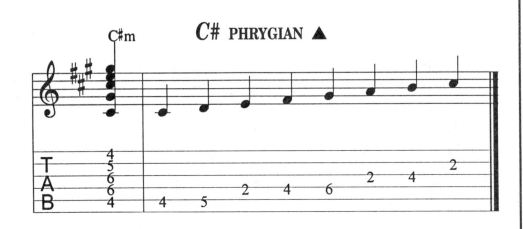

ILLUSTRATION TWO (37) *CHA CHA   TEMPO 124*

STUDY EXERCISE

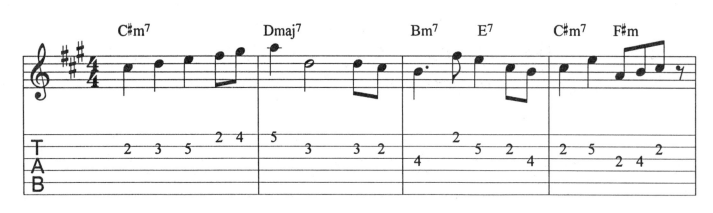

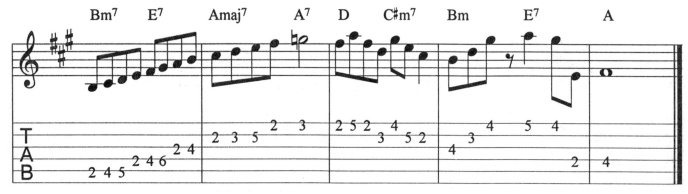

< 79 >

MODES DERIVED FROM MAJOR SCALES

ILLUSTRATION ONE

Form Three
G Scale Pattern

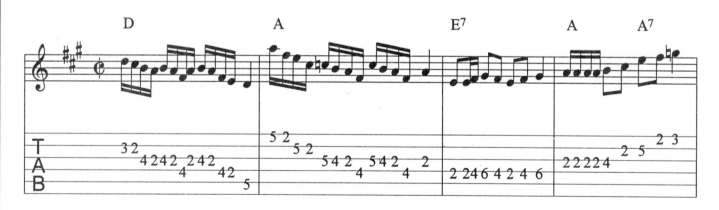

LYDIAN MODE
Fourth Degree

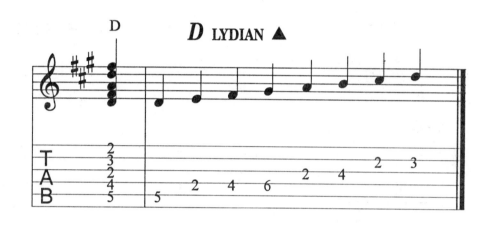

ILLUSTRATION TWO   (38)   *CAJUN BEAT TEMPO 120*

STUDY EXERCISE

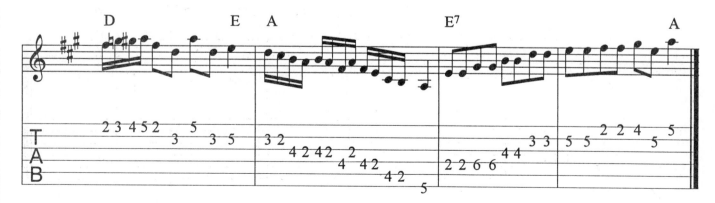

MODES DERIVED FROM MAJOR SCALES

ILLUSTRATION ONE

MIXOLYDIAN MODE
Fifth Degree

Form Three
G Scale Pattern

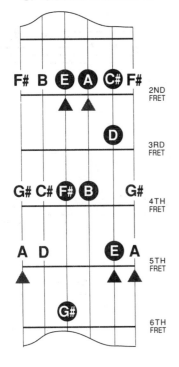

ILLUSTRATION TWO (39) *ROCK BEAT TEMPO 155*

STUDY EXERCISE

< 81 >

MODES DERIVED FROM MAJOR SCALES

ILLUSTRATION ONE

Form Three
G Scale Pattern

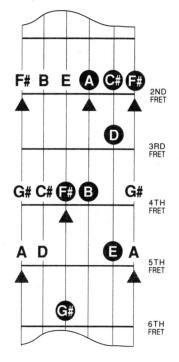

AEOLIAN MODE
Sixth Degree

A MAJOR SCALE ▲

AEOLIAN

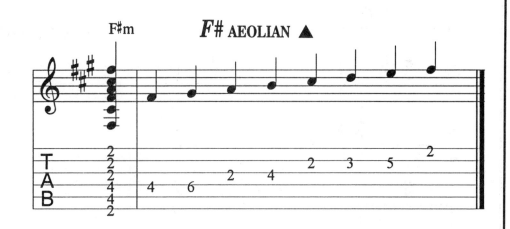

F# AEOLIAN ▲

ILLUSTRATION TWO

ROCK BEAT TEMPO 155

STUDY EXERCISE

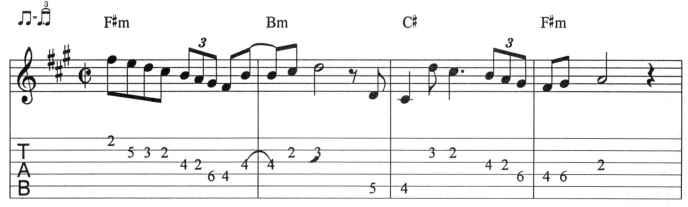

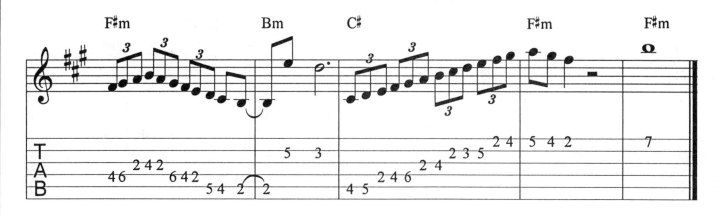

< 82 >

MODES DERIVED FROM MAJOR SCALES

ILLUSTRATION ONE

Form Three
G Scale Pattern

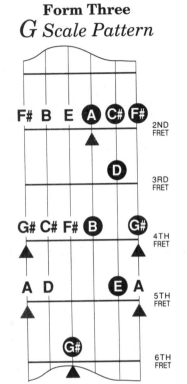

LOCRIAN MODE
Seventh Degree

A MAJOR SCALE ▲

G# LOCRIAN ▲

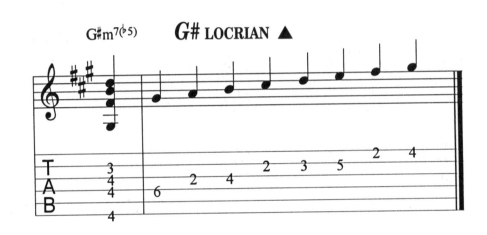

ILLUSTRATION TWO (41) *RHUMBA TEMPO 140*

STUDY EXERCISE

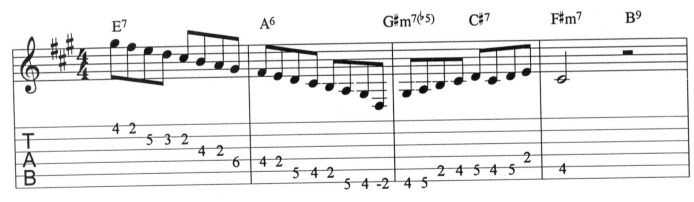

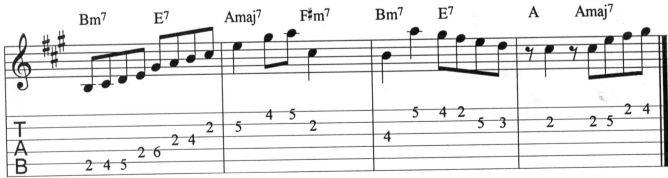

MODES DERIVED FROM MAJOR SCALES

ILLUSTRATION ONE

DORIAN MODE
Second Degree

Form Four
E Scale Pattern

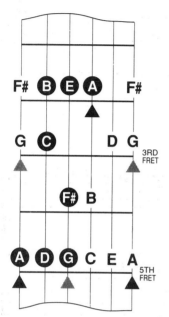

ILLUSTRATION TWO *FUNK TEMPO 145*

STUDY EXERCISE

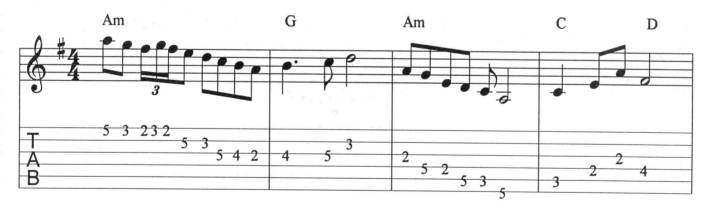

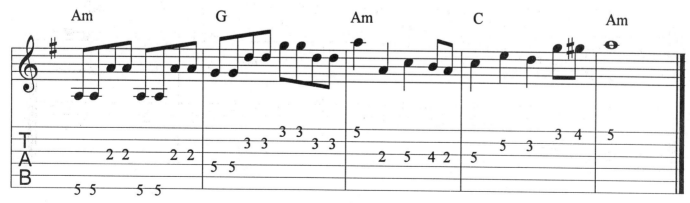

< 84 >

MODES DERIVED FROM MAJOR SCALES

ILLUSTRATION ONE

PHRYGIAN MODE
Third Degree

Form Four
E Scale Pattern

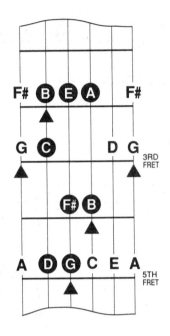

G MAJOR SCALE ▲

LYDIAN

B PHRYGIAN ▲

ILLUSTRATION TWO (43) *POP ROCK TEMPO 124*

STUDY EXERCISE

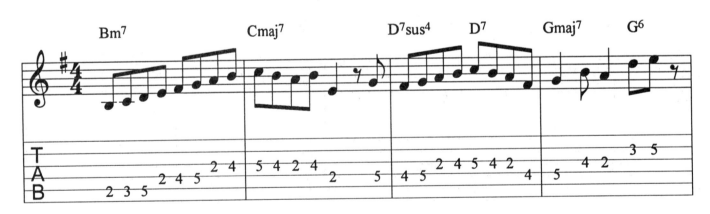

MODES DERIVED FROM MAJOR SCALES

ILLUSTRATION ONE

Form Four
E Scale Pattern

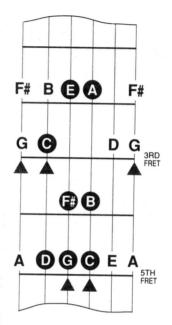

LYDIAN MODE
Fourth Degree

G MAJOR SCALE ▲

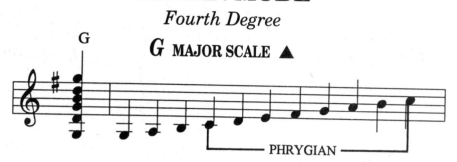

PHRYGIAN

C LYDIAN ▲

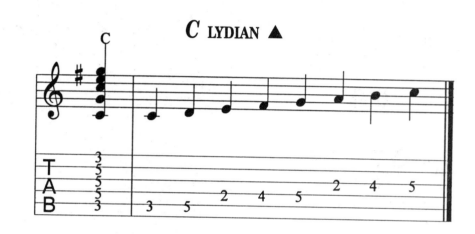

ILLUSTRATION TWO (44) LAMBADA TEMPO 126

STUDY EXERCISE

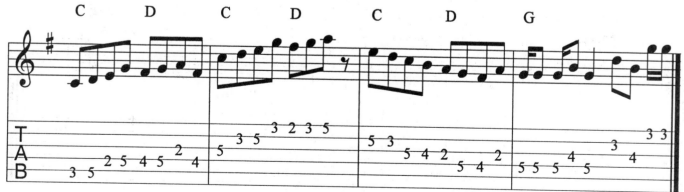

< 86 >

MODES DERIVED FROM MAJOR SCALES

ILLUSTRATION ONE

Form Four
E Scale Pattern

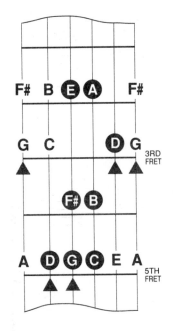

MIXOLYDIAN MODE
Fifth Degree

G MAJOR SCALE ▲

D MIXOLYDIAN ▲

ILLUSTRATION TWO ㊺ *ROCK N' ROLL BALLAD TEMPO 134*

STUDY EXERCISE

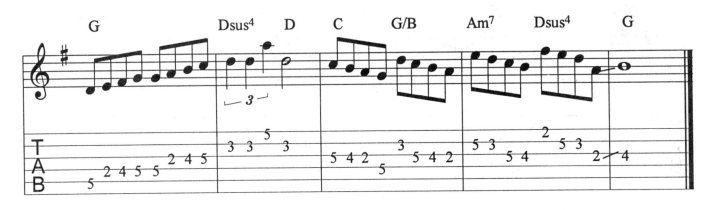

< 87 >

MODES DERIVED FROM MAJOR SCALES

ILLUSTRATION ONE

Form Four
E Scale Pattern

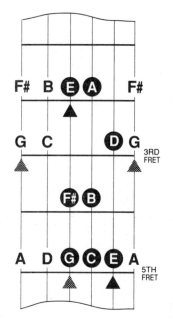

AEOLIAN MODE
Sixth Degree

G MAJOR SCALE ▲

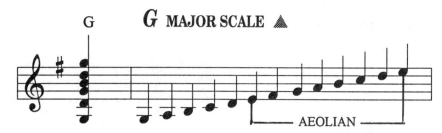

E AEOLIAN ▲

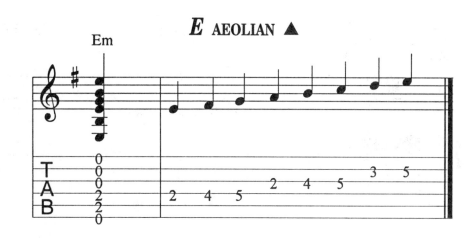

ILLUSTRATION TWO (46) *BOSSANOVA TEMPO 150*

STUDY EXERCISE

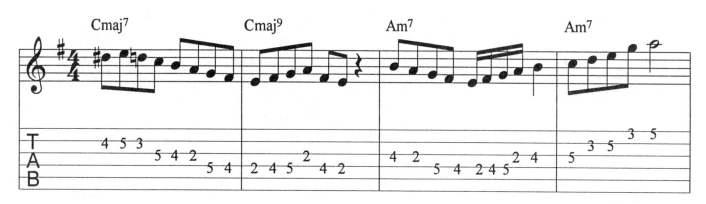

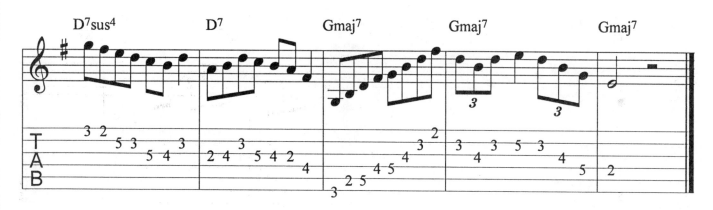

MODES DERIVED FROM MAJOR SCALES

ILLUSTRATION ONE

Form Four
E Scale Pattern

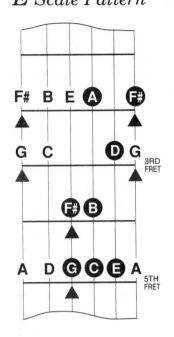

LOCRIAN MODE
Seventh Degree

G MAJOR SCALE ▲

LOCRIAN

F#m⁷⁽♭⁵⁾   **F#** LOCRIAN ▲

ILLUSTRATION TWO (47) *SWING TEMPO 150*

STUDY EXERCISE

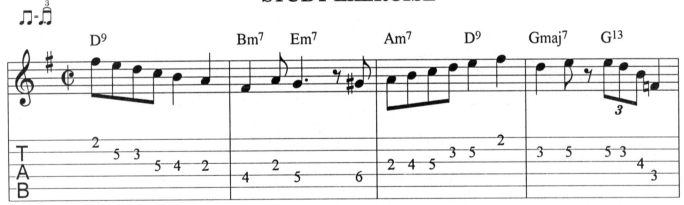

D⁹   Bm⁷ Em⁷   Am⁷   D⁹   Gmaj⁷   G¹³

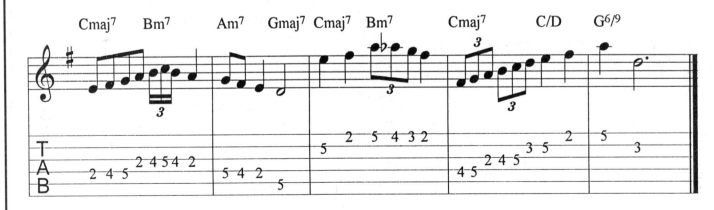

Cmaj⁷ Bm⁷   Am⁷ Gmaj⁷ Cmaj⁷ Bm⁷   Cmaj⁷   C/D   G⁶ᐟ⁹

< 89 >

MODES DERIVED FROM MAJOR SCALES

ILLUSTRATION ONE

Form Five

D Scale Pattern

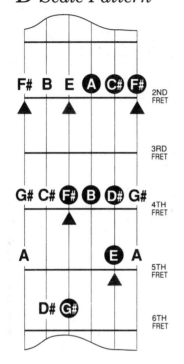

DORIAN MODE
Second Degree

E   *E* MAJOR SCALE ▲

DORIAN

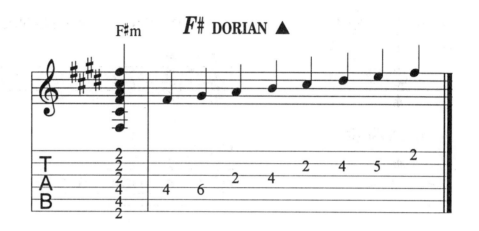

F#m   *F#* DORIAN ▲

ILLUSTRATION TWO (48) *ROCK BEAT TEMPO 155*

STUDY EXERCISE

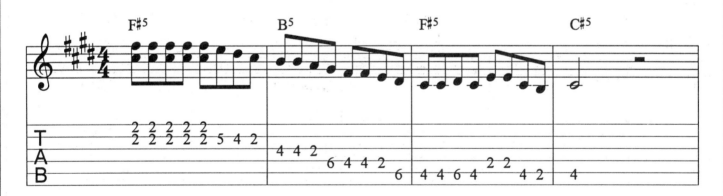

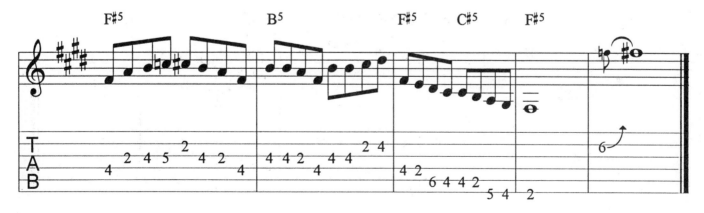

MODES DERIVED FROM MAJOR SCALES

ILLUSTRATION ONE

Form Five
D Scale Pattern

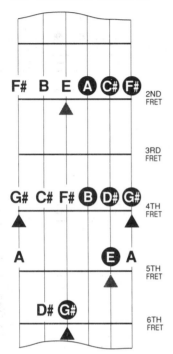

PHRYGIAN MODE
Third Degree

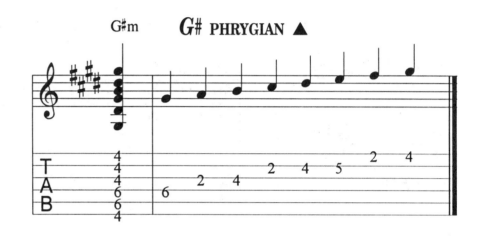

ILLUSTRATION TWO

(49) *ALTERNATIVE TEMPO 125*

STUDY EXERCISE

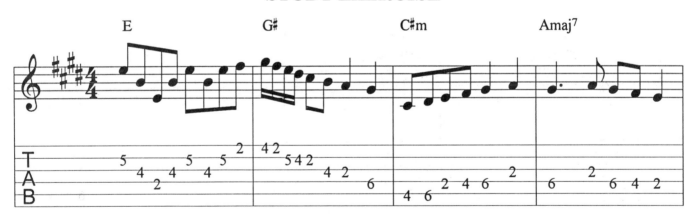

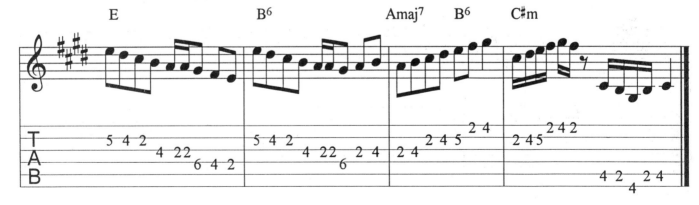

< 91 >

MODES DERIVED FROM MAJOR SCALES

ILLUSTRATION ONE

Form Five
D Scale Pattern

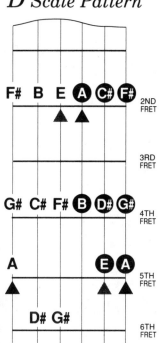

LYDIAN MODE
Fourth Degree

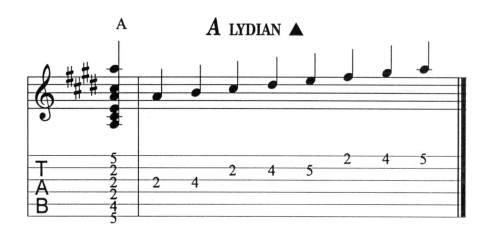

E — **E MAJOR SCALE ▲**

LYDIAN

A — **A LYDIAN ▲**

ILLUSTRATION TWO (50) *COUNTRY WALTZ 122*

STUDY EXERCISE

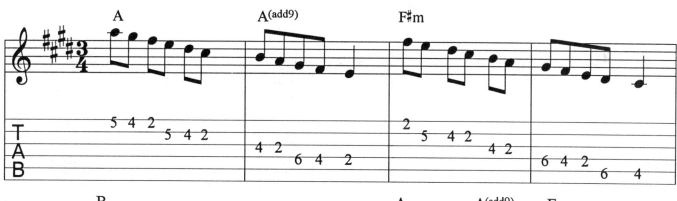

< 92 >

MODES DERIVED FROM MAJOR SCALES

ILLUSTRATION ONE

Form Five
D Scale Pattern

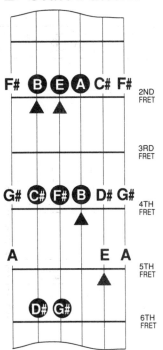

MIXOLYDIAN MODE
Fifth Degree

E MAJOR SCALE ▲

B MIXOLYDIAN ▲

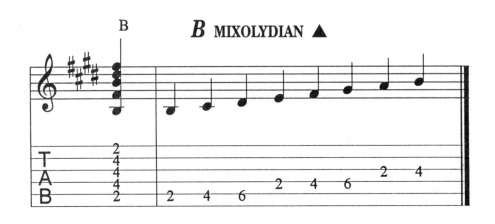

ILLUSTRATION TWO (51) *HARD ROCK TEMPO 122*

STUDY EXERCISE

B⁷sus⁴   B   E   E⁷sus⁴

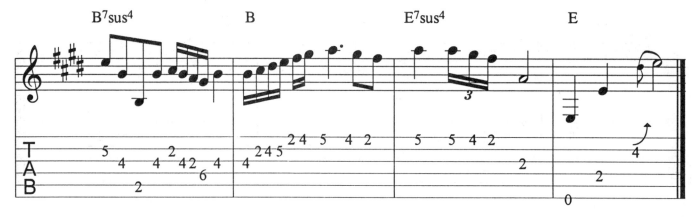

B⁷sus⁴   B   E⁷sus⁴   E

< 93 >

MODES DERIVED FROM MAJOR SCALES

ILLUSTRATION ONE

Form Five
D Scale Pattern

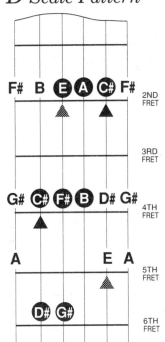

AEOLIAN MODE
Sixth Degree

E MAJOR SCALE ▲

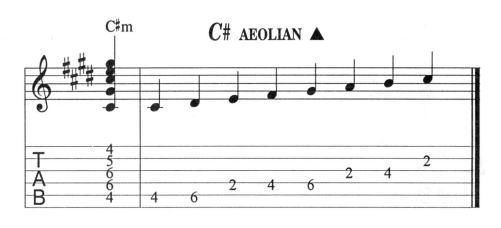

C# AEOLIAN ▲

ILLUSTRATION TWO 〔52〕 *BEGUINE TEMPO 140*

STUDY EXERCISE

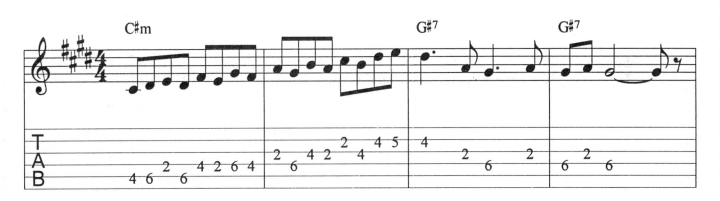

< 94 >

MODES DERIVED FROM MAJOR SCALES

ILLUSTRATION ONE

Form Five
D Scale Pattern

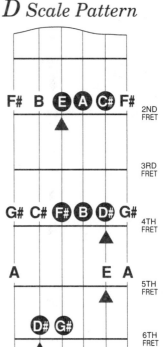

LOCRIAN MODE
Seventh Degree

E MAJOR SCALE ▲

D♯ LOCRIAN ▲

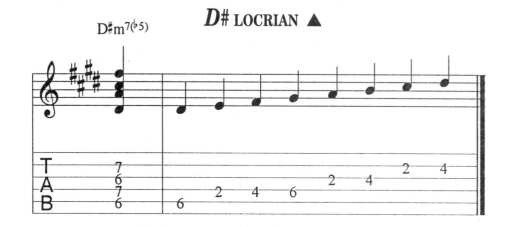

ILLUSTRATION TWO (53) *16 BEAT TEMPO 77*

STUDY EXERCISE

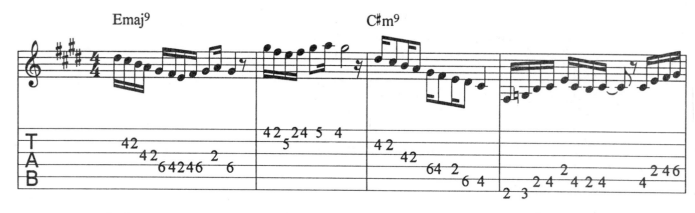

< 95 >

MODAL INDEX

(24)	*E* Dorian	Bossanova	Tempo 105
(25)	*F#* Phrygian	Oldies	Tempo 135
(26)	*G* Lydian	Rock Beat	Tempo 135
(27)	*A* Mixolydian	Country Beat	Tempo 119
(28)	*B* Aeolian	Rap Beat	Tempo 94
(29)	*C#* Locrian	6/8 Beat	Tempo 68
(30)	*D* Dorian	Rock Beat	Tempo 130
(31)	*E* Phrygian	16 Beat Feel	Tempo 118
(32)	*F* Lydian	Hard Rock	Tempo 122
(33)	*G* Mixolydian	Oldies Rock	Tempo 178
(34)	*A* Aeolian	Brush Swing	Tempo 122
(35)	*B* Locrian	Lambada	Tempo 126
(36)	*B* Dorian	Rhythm & Blues	Tempo 110
(37)	*C#* Phrygian	Cha Cha	Tempo 124
(38)	*D* Lydian	Cajun Beat	Tempo 120
(39)	*E* Mixolydian	Waltz	Tempo 214
(40)	*F#* Aeolian	Rock Shuffle	Tempo 156
(41)	*G#* Locrian	Rumba	Tempo 140
(42)	*A* Dorian	Funk	Tempo 148
(43)	*B* Phrygian	Pop Rock	Tempo 124
(44)	*C* Lydian	Lambada	Tempo 126
(45)	*D* Mixolydian	Rock & Roll Ballad	Tempo 134
(46)	*E* Aeolian	Bossanova	Tempo 150
(47)	*F#* Locrian	Swing	Tempo 150
(48)	*F#* Dorian	Rock Beat	Tempo 155
(49)	*G#* Phrygian	Alternative	Tempo 125
(50)	*A* Lydian	Country Waltz	Tempo 122
(51)	*B* Mixolydian	Hard Rock	Tempo 121
(52)	*C#* Aeolian	Beguine	Tempo 140
(53)	*D#* Locrian	16 Beat	Tempo 77

< 96 >

MODAL PLAYING

section four REVIEW

─── STREET SMARTS ───

Modal improvisation is as simple as playing a diatonic scale!

─── PAGE 61 ───

─── STREET SMARTS ───

Knowing where to start a scale within the diatonic fingering pattern is the KEY to improvisation. You must know what notes form each chord, and where these notes lay within the scale pattern. With this knowledge, you will be able to improvise by playing modes and you always play correct notes!

─── PAGE 62 ───

─── STREET SMARTS ───

Traditional modal studies require you to memorize scale formulas (step / half-step patterns), and over the chord each mode may be played. This is boring and confusing to novice players. We ask you to learn the notes that form the chords you commonly use, or better yet, learn how to instinctively count, in thirds, and determine triads in your head.

─── PAGE 65 ───

< 97 >

section five

TRIADIC IMPROVISATION

Now, we put together all the accumulated knowledge you have gained from your study of this book and begin our excursion into creating lead lines over chord progressions. Now the fun begins! If you have not already purchased the Audio Companion cassette tape, we recommend you do so at this time, for it is only by practicing with a band that you be able to put into effective use the knowledge you will acquire.

SELF-CONFIDENCE IS FAITH IN YOURSELF

Believe you have the ability to achieve the objective you desire. Do not procrastinate. Do today everything you can to further develop your skills. It is in this manner you will, slowly but inevitably, develop self-confidence.

< 98 >

TRIADIC IMPROVISATION
PLAYING FROM CHORD TRIADS

RULES OF TRIADIC IMPROVISATION

Previously we asked that you learn chord triads, the notes that form each chord, in all keys. We have explained that this is the centerpiece of our approach to improvisation. It is now time to define the term, "Triadic Improvisation". In its simplistic form, Triadic Improvisation is playing specific parallel scales built from within a parent scale. Parent scale is defined as the key signature scale, or the scale that harmonizes a set group of chords within a progression (See Key Centers). We often refer to the note upon which we begin this new scale as a "Guide Tone". These new scales are chosen to harmonize individual chords over which we are improvising a solo. These new scales may commence on any note of the chord triad, Triadic Improvisation. The scales thus created are referred to as Modes and their usage is called Model Playing.

In summary: We can play correct lead patterns, patterns that will harmonize the melody, by simply knowing the chord being played, beginning a scale on any note of a chords triad, and playing only parent scale notes.

The term triad means three. In chord construction this is the Root (1), 3rd, and 5th notes of the scale. This in effect provides us with three different scale we may play over a chord. Are there rules to determine which should be used? As you progress with your study of improvisation you will develop a better understanding of modal usage and we will explore additional improvisational technique and rules, but for now we will simply suggest starting the new scale (mode) on the Root note of the chord.

At this time we must distinguish between diatonic and non-diatonic chords and how this effects the rules of improvisation. Our studies are based on diatonic chords, those chords containing only notes of the parent scale. Non-diatonic chords contain altered notes, a flat fifth, sharp ninth etc.,. It is important to realize that altered chords require altered scales. This will be further defined later in this book, but for now we concentrate on diatonic harmony, scales, and chords.

ILLUSTRATION ONE

The Triadic Harmonization Chart is the most significant instructional aid you will encounter in your study of improvisation. It represents the most important aspect of this book. Learn to apply it to your playing and you will always be able to create instant solos, and you will always play notes that harmonize with the rhythm chords. The chart presents the major diatonic scale harmonized in thirds. It shows each degree, its triad (the three notes formed by harmonizing in thirds), and the resulting chord name. Below each chord we place the name of each triad note (guide tone) and its scale degree number. The chart can be used as a handy reference guide until you can readily recall the triad of each chord being used. When the chord changes, simply start another lead pattern from one the new chord"s triad notes, again playing only notes of the parent scale. (Remember, we are utilizing diatonic chords, diatonic scale patterns).

We are, at this time, only familiarizing you with the basic principal of improvising note patterns from the scale. There are many other aspects of improvisation that must be understood and fully mastered before you can create "exciting" solos, or even workable "fills", "licks", and "phrases". But first you must become familiar with the musical rules of scales and arpeggios.

On the following pages we complete our explanation of triadic improvisation, and we further explain how to use the Triadic Harmonization Chart.

NOTE: At the back of this book we provide Triadic Harmonization Charts written in all of the more commonly used keys.

< 99 >

TRIAD HARMONIZATION CHART

Key of *C* Major

ILLUSTRATION ONE

KEY OF *C* MAJOR

DEGREE	I	ii	iii	IV	V	Vi	Vii	I
CHORD	C	Dm	Em	F	G	Am	Bm b5	C

Triad	G E C	A F D	B G E	C A F	F D B G	E C A	F D B	G E C

**REMEMBER: A SCALE PLAYED FORM ANY NOTE OF A CHORD TRIAD
(GUIDE TONES) WILL HARMONIZE THE CHORD.**

< 100 >

TRIADIC IMPROVISATION

MODAL PLAYING

IMPROVISING OVER MAJOR DIATONIC CHORDS

We will now put into use the KEY element presented in this book. We will play scales over rhythm chords. The scales starting notes are determined by the triad of the chord over which we play our lead lines. Our rhythm pattern, at this time, is comprised of only one chord and we have selected individual scale position for the convenience of writing each exercises in Tablature. We encourage you to play the exercises from each of the five scale patterns we use in this book. To be successful at improvisation, you must learn to use all five patterns.

ILLUSTRATION ONE

RHYTHM CHART – KEY OF *C* MAJOR

We include the rhythm chart for you convenience. If you have not purchased the accompanying 𝒶udio 𝒞ompanion, have a friend play this chart as you practice the exercises. We have written the *C* chord triad so you will know upon which note in the *C* Major Scale you can play a parallel scale, a mode. We include the Mode name to help familiarize you with modal terminology. This exercise is performed with the form one open "C" scale pattern.

ILLUSTRATION TWO

IONIAN MODE – NOTE *C*

This four bar exercise presents the *C* scale. A scale beginning on the first note of a major scale is an Ionian Mode.

ILLUSTRATION THREE

PHRYGIAN MODE – NOTE *E*

This exercise starts on the 3rd of the *C* chord triad, the *E* note. A scale beginning on the third note of a major scale is a Phrygian Mode.

ILLUSTRATION FOUR

MIXOLYDIAN MODE – NOTE *G*

This exercise starts on the 5th of the *C* chord triad, the *G* note. A scale beginning on the fifth note of a major scale is a Mixolydian Mode.

< 101 >

IMPROVISING OVER MAJOR CHORDS

ILLUSTRATION ONE

RHYTHM CHART (54)
Key of *C* Major

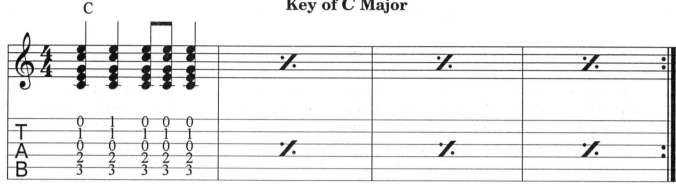

ILLUSTRATION TWO

**SCALE STARTING ON
TONIC NOTE "C" (Ionian Mode)**

ILLUSTRATION THREE

**SCALE STARTING ON
3RD NOTE "E" (Phrygian Mode)**

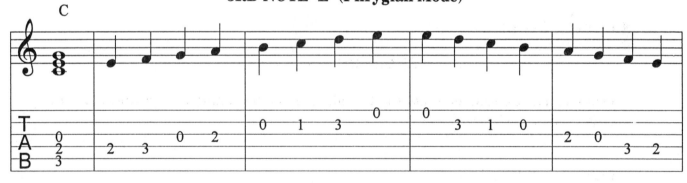

ILLUSTRATION FOUR

**SCALE STARTING ON
5TH NOTE "G" (Mixolydian Mode)**

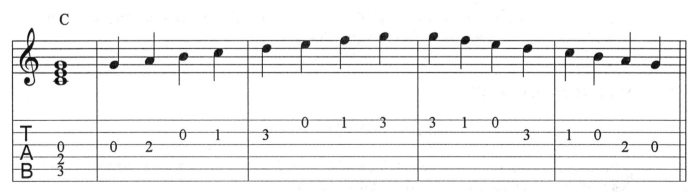

TRIADIC IMPROVISATION

IMPROVISING OVER DIATONIC MINOR CHORDS

MODAL PLAYING

IMPROVISING OVER DIATONIC MINOR CHORDS

ILLUSTRATION ONE

Rhythm chart – key of *C Major*, (*D Minor* chord). We include the rhythm chart for your convenience. Again, if your do not have the Audio Companion for this book, have a friend play the chart as you practice the exercise. We have written the *D Minor* chord triad so you will know upon which triad note of the *D Minor* chord you can play a parallel scale. We include the Mode name to familiarize you with modal terminology. This exercise is performed with the "C", form one open pattern. Practice playing these exercises from other patterns.

ILLUSTRATION TWO

DORIAN MODE – NOTE *D*

This four bar exercise present the *D Minor* chord. A scale beginning on the second note of a major scale is called a DORIAN mode.

ILLUSTRATION THREE

LYDIAN MODE – NOTE *F*

This exercise starts on the 3rd of the *D Minor* chord, the note *F*. A scale beginning on the third note of a *D Minor* chord is the FOURTH note of the parent scale, in this example, *C Major*. A mode played from the fourth degree of a major scale is called a LYDIAN mode.

ILLUSTRATION FOUR

AEOLIAN MODE – NOTE *A*

This exercise starts on the 5th of the *D Minor* chord, the note *A*. A scale beginning on the fifth note of a *D Minor* chord is the SIXTH note of the parent scale, in this example, *C Major*. A mode played from the 6th degree of a major scale is called an AEOLEAN mode.

IMPROVISING OVER MINOR CHORDS

ILLUSTRATION ONE **RHYTHM CHART** 55
Key of *C*

ILLUSTRATION TWO **SCALE STARTING ON**
TONIC NOTE "D" (Dorian Mode)

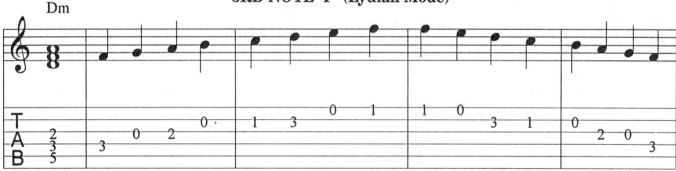

ILLUSTRATION THREE **SCALE STARTING ON**
3RD NOTE "F" (Lydian Mode)

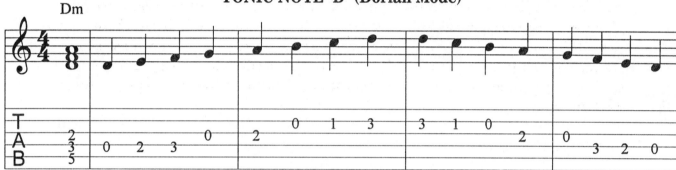

ILLUSTRATION FOUR **SCALE STARTING ON**
5TH NOTE "A" (Aeolian Mode)

TRIAD IMPROVISATION

KEY CENTERS

While the key signature does establish the rules we must use when playing a melody, strange things happen when we begin to improvise. Writers and arrangers frequently incorporate non-diatonic tones, accidentals (sharps-flats) in order to move a melody along in a desired direction. This in turn can create chords out side the original scale. This occurs because individual chords appear in more then one key. The use of accidentals also creates non-diatonic harmony which in turn requires non-diatonic chords to be used. The chords are created by adding a note not within the scale specified by the key signature.

It is for these reasons chord progressions may modulate to various keys, often without any clue to the musician, except perhaps for accidentals that appear in the melody, or the appearance of non-diatonic chords. This change of key center, implied or real, is usually created by the choice of chords that appear within the chord progression.

Our study of "Scales Over Chords" has been focused on individual chord harmony and playing scales from individual notes of each triad. You have been able to concentrate on playing all scales from one fingering pattern, the original key signature scale. This one-by-one chord technique has its creative limitations.

If we learn to associate chord groups by the scale (key) of which they are formulated, we allow ourselves alternatives that permit full exploration of our improvisational potential.

UNDERSTANDING CHORD GROUPS

ILLUSTRATION ONE

Determining key centers is simply a matter of identifying a chord sequence as belonging to a specific scale. It is most important to understand that you CANNOT determine the scale of which a chord belongs by isolating individual chords within a progression. Why? Because specific chords are found in more than one key (scale).

In Illustration One, we show the C Major scale harmonized in third intervals (Triads). If you have memorized scale harmony as presented previously, you know that each key produces seven chords which fall into three chord types: Two Major chords, the first and fourth degrees; three minor chords, the second, third, and sixth degrees; and one dominant seventh, the fifth degree. (The seventh degree may be used either as a minor or diminished chord).

ILLUSTRATION TWO

A study of keys will demonstrate that chords may appear in more then one key. Major chords appear in two different keys, the three minors, in four keys. The dominant seventh will only appear in one key, it is always the fifth of the parent scale.

< 105 >

C MAJOR SCALE–SEVENTH CHORDS

ILLUSTRATION ONE
Key of *C* Major

DOMINANT SEVENTH

Chords	C	Dm	Em	F	G7	Am	Bm b5	C
Keys Chords Appear In	C F	F Bb C Dm	C D G Em	F C Bb	C	G F C Am		C F

ILLUSTRATION TWO

CHORDS BY KEYS

Major Chords		Keys		Minor Chords		Keys			Dominant Chords	Keys
C	C	G	F	Cmi	Cmi	D#	G#	A#	C7	F
D	D	A	G	Dmi	Dmi	F	A#	C	D7	G
E	E	B	A	Emi	Emi	G	C	D	E7	A
F	F	C	Bb	Fmi	Fmi	G#	C#	D#	F7	Bb
G	G	D	C	Gmi	Gmi	A#	D#	F	G7	C
A	A	E	D	Ami	Ami	C	F	G	A7	D
B	B	F#	E	Bmi	Bmi	D	G	A	B7	E

< 106 >

IDENTIFYING CHORD GROUPS
WITHIN PROGRESSIONS

Our studies, until now, have concentrated on learning to play specific scales over individual chords. We now focus on identifying chord progressions (a progression is the order in which chords appear within a song), and specifically, those short sets of chords called *chord groups*, as belonging to one common scale.

To improvise effectively, it is necessary to play a scale common to these connecting chords so we can develop our melodic melodies and musical statements without interruptions or the need to adjust to new guide tone for each chord. Example: *F, G7, C* are the three primary chords that harmonize the *C* Major scale and we may play a *C* scale over these chords. *Bb, C7, F* harmonize the *F* Major scale and we may play an *F* scale over these chords. Having identified the key of which a group of chords belong, we can then determine the correct scale pattern, shift the starting note (guide tone) to match the chord group, and then use our improvisational tools (arpeggios, common tones and modes) to create effective solos. The examples on the following pages are considered "common" chord groups. Learn to identify them and instantly know the parent scale of which they belong, so you can improvise solo lead lines without fear of stumbling or playing bad notes.

THE IV-V-I PROGRESSION

Each chord has its own distinct effect upon the tonality of a chord progression of which it is a part. Of the seven chords (Diatonic Scale Harmony), the three most important chords, called the primary chords, are the Tonic (I), the Subdominant (IV), and the Dominant (V). This occurs because chords built on the fourth (IV) and fifth (V) degrees are, like the Tonic (I), comprised of major triads. The IV and V appearance establishes a strong gravitation to the tonic chord. This chord group is enough to indicate the key of which a composition is written. Seeing the chords *C, D, G* (written example, following page) establishes the song as being in the key of *G* Major. The IV-V-I progression is the cornerstone of traditional harmony and is used extensively in Country and Rock chord progressions (see páge 45).

<107>

IV-V-I PROGRESSION

STUDY EXERCISE (56) *LAMBADA TEMPO 126*

Example 56 is written in the key of *G* Major (key signature-one sharp). However, the song starts on the fourth note of the scale (the note *C*), and is harmonized with the sub-dominant chord, *C* Major. A mode starting on the fourth note of a Diatonic scale is a Lydian mode. Therefore, the song begins with a *C* Lydian mode. Measure two is simply a *D* chord arpeggio, and measure three is a *G* Major scale (the parent scale). Measure four is another arpeggio. Measures five and six are simply scale movements. Measure seven is a Phrygian mode, while measure eight is again, an arpeggio movement. Each measure starts with a note of the chord triad that harmonizes that measure. Study exercise 56 is played from the *G* scale, pattern four. We encourage you to experiment with your own lead line, and practice this exercise in all five patterns. We also suggest beginning your improvised solos from other triad notes.

NOTE: In our example, we have included extra measures to show the triad of each chord used. These *triadic measures* are not to be played and are not counted. This may be confusing at first, since the placement of the chord triad (written in whole notes), creates split measures (the triads appear in the middle of a measure). However, we feel it is a helpful instructional aid at this point in your studies of triadic improvisation.

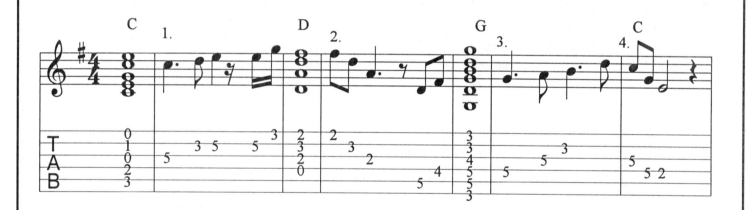

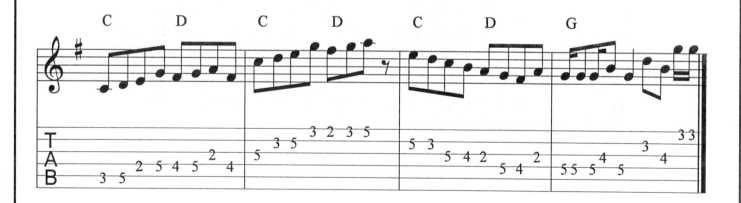

IDENTIFYING CHORD GROUPS
WITHIN PROGRESSIONS

THE ii-V-I PROGRESSION

Triads built on the second (ii), third (iii) and sixth (vi) degrees of the major scale form minor chords, called secondary chords. Because several major and minor chords within a key are similar in triadic composition (they share two of the three notes that form their triads), minor chords are used freely in substitution for major chords with which it shares common tones.

The ii chord (minor), played as a ii7 seventh, is often substituted for the IV in modern chord progressions. In the key of C Major, the IV chord (F Major) is comprised of the notes F-A-C, and the ii minor seventh is comprised of the notes D-F-A-C. Since only the note D distinguished the Dmi7 from its companion Major chord, F Major, the ii7 is often used in direct substitution for the IV chord. This gives us the common progression of ii7-V-I. This combination (Dmi7-G7-C) is enough to indicate that the key center is C Major, and the proper parent scale to play over these chords is the C Major scale. Having established the correct scale, we may then concentrate on creating our solo by first choosing our starting tone, or guide tone (Triadic Improvisation), from the appropriate scale pattern. The guide tone may be any of the chord triad tones. The ii7-V chord group proceeding a I chord, signals a new chord group.

Passing Tones

Passing tones are notes that appear in the melody that are not common to a chord's triadic composition, and they occur from playing a scale over a chord group. These notes are called accidentals and function to create a smooth melodic passage from one chord to another. They are usually quick notes in duration (eighth notes, sixteenth notes, etc.). In exercise 57, they occur in the second, fourth, sixth and seventh measures.

<109>

ii-V-I PROGRESSION

STUDY EXERCISE (57) *POP ROCK TEMPO 130*

ANALYSIS

We begin exercise 57, measure one, with a *D* Dorian mode played over the *Dmi7* chord. A mode commencing on the second note of the parent scale is called a Dorian Mode; in the key of *C* major, *D* Dorian. We continue the *D* Dorian mode over the *G7* chord, second measure. In the third and fourth measures, we use an *A* Aeolean mode (sixth scale step). The next five measures are variations of the previous four. Brackets identify the ii7-V7-I chord group. Our exercise is played from the *A* pattern, form two.

NOTE: Again, we use triadic measure to show the chord triads. They are not to be counted nor played.

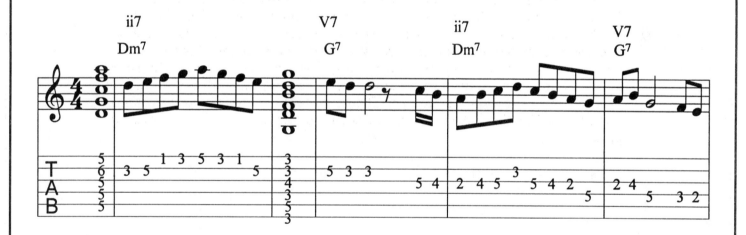

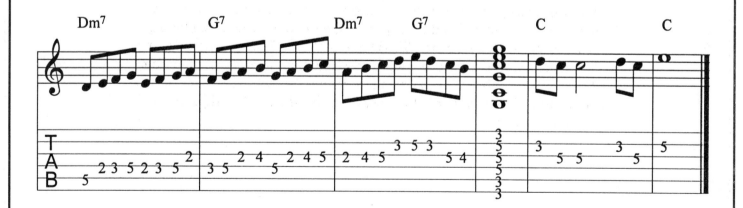

< 110 >

vi-IV-V-I PROGRESSION

The vi-IV-V-I progression is another chord group that is easily recognizable. (We have placed a bracket over this progression in our excercise). A soloist must learn to identify these groups through a thoughtful analysis of each song and instinctively know what pattern or scale is most appropriate to facilitate ease of playing and allow you to maintain the integrity of the melody. Again, we must stress that identifying a scale common to a group of chords as belonging to one key center will simplify the creation or your solo lines.

The V-I chord group establishes a key center. However, it is advisable to determine if any preceding chords are also common with this sub-chord group. In the 1950-60's, the use of the relative minor chord as part of this group came into common practice and helped to establish the musical sounds of that era – it is still popular to this day. The relative minor, a chord built on the sixth note of the scale, is often used in substitution for the Tonic chord because their triads share two notes in common. The relative minor's "tonal sound" has a natural tendency to gravitate towards the IV chord which as we already know, pulls to the V7 chord and then on to the I chord (page 45). This "feel of tonal rotation" makes this chord group most useful in composing songs and solos.

The vi-IV-V-I chord sub group defines the key center of the I chord.

< 111 >

vi-IV-V7-I PROGRESSION

STUDY EXERCISE 58 TEMPO 65

Exercise 58 is in the key of *G* (one sharp) and played out of the *G* pattern, form three. The first chord (measure one) is the Tonic chord, *G* major, followed by *E* minor (second measure). In the key of *G* major, the *E* note is the sixth note of the scale, and a chord built on the sixth is a minor chord called the relative minor (vi). The lead pattern for this measure also begins on the sixth note of the scale (note *E*) and a mode played from the sixth note is called an Aeolian mode. (The Aeolian mode is the mode of choice to play over the relative minor chord.) Measure three is harmonized with the subdominant chord (1V) *C* major. The lead pattern begins on the root note of the *C* Major chord, the note *C*, which is the fourth note of the *G* major scale. A mode commencing on the fourth note of a diatonic scale is called a Lydian mode. Measure four is harmonized with the Dominant Seventh chord, which in the key of *G* major, is *D7*. Our lead pattern commences on the note A, the fifth of the *D7* chord triad which is the second note of the *G* major scale. A mode played from the second note of a *G* major scale creates an *A* Dorian mode. All the chords used in Exercise 58 are *G* scale chords – that is, chords formed by harmonizing the *G* major scale in third intervals. Therefore, all our modal playing utilizes only notes of the *G* major scale.

REMEMBER: Do not play the triadic measures!

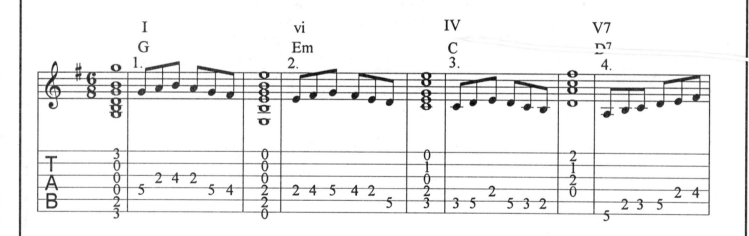

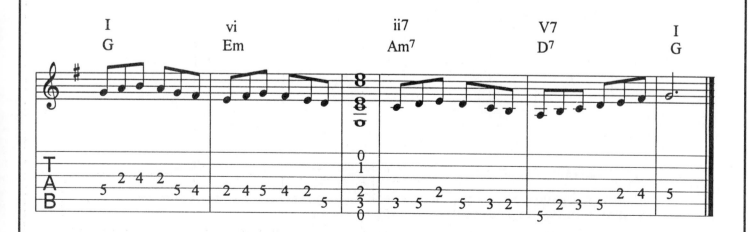

TRIADIC IMPROVISATION

IDENTIFYING CHORD GROUPS
WITHIN PROGRESSIONS

In our study of diatonic harmony, we stressed the importance of understanding the relationship between the dominant chord (V) and the Tonic (1). It is from the scale they share in common (the parent scale), that we build our modes. To improvise effectively over dominant chords, we must quickly determine the dominant chord's parent scale; and this may be accomplished by a device called the "circle of fourths" (page 19). In essence, we simply count up (alphabetically) four intervals. Example: *E9*, a dominant chord. To determine the parent scale of this chord, we may count up four notes: *E F G A*. The *E9* chord is the dominant chord (V) of the *A* major scale. The fifth note of the *A* major scale is the note *E*, and by playing a scale from this note, we create an *E* Mixolydian mode.

Exercise 59 is a study in playing Mixolydian modes over a series of dominant type chords where each chord creates its own key center; and we also introduce you to chord substitution. We use major chords (raised third in triad) for substation for the minor iii-vi-ii chords. This creates a chord progression made up of major chords (III7-VI7-II7-V7-I). Since each chord is a dominant type chord, you must quickly determine the chord's parent scale, then play from the fifth note to play the correct Mixolydian mode.

REMEMBER: Do not play or count the triadic measures!

STUDY EXERCISE 59 *LAMBADA TEMPO 126*

┌─ **PRACTICE TIP** ────────────────────────────────────

E9 – E Mixolydian, *B7* – B Mixolydian, *A7* – A Mixolydian. See if you can determine which scale pattern is being used over each chord.

< 113 >

III7-VI7-II7-V7-I PROGRESSION

< 114 >

TRIADIC IMPROVISATION

Exercise 60 is a study of the ii7-V7-I chord group used as device to change and identify new key centers within a written piece of music. With help of brackets, we have grouped all the chords together into their proper key centers. The use of the Dorian mode is always an effective improvisational device over the ii7-V7-I chord group. Notice in this arrangement how this chord group signals each new key center and our usage of the Dorian mode over this chord group.

STUDY EXERCISE 60 SOUL BALLAD TEMPO 105

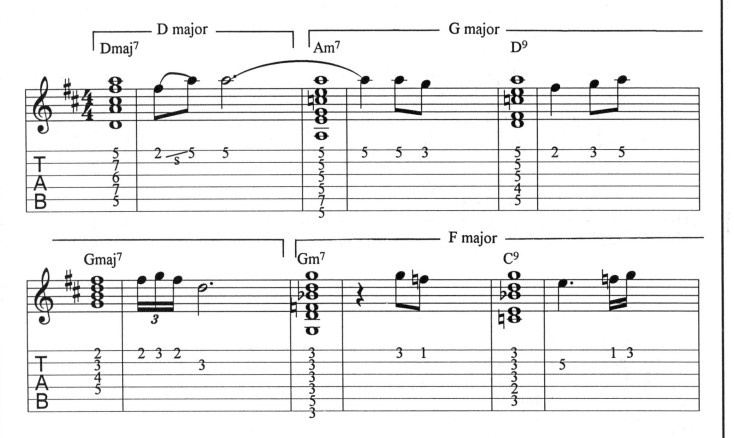

< 115 >

STUDY EXERCISE 60

Study exercise 60 continued

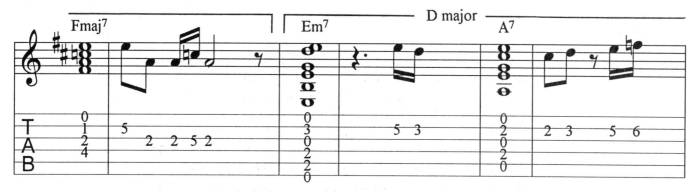

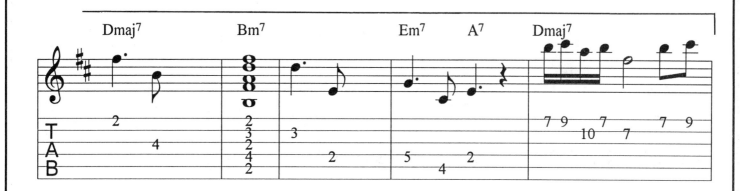

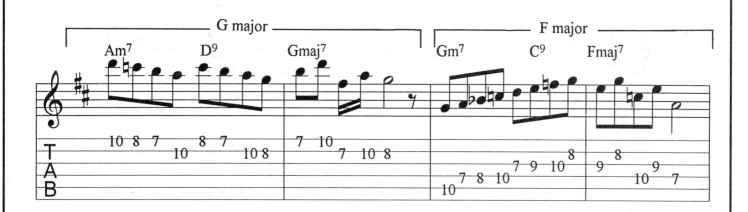

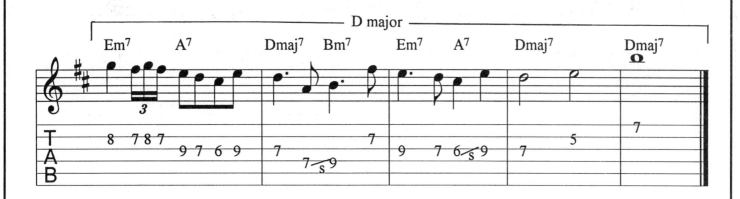

< 116 >

TRIADIC IMPROVISATION

Exercise 61 brings together all aspects of improvisational playing as previously explained in this book. It is a full, written arrangement utilizing many of the elements of music composition (explained below), that a soloist will encounter playing with a band.

Introduction – A short phrase (riff) which prepares the way for the main body of a composition.
Verse – Part of a composition that often comes after the introduction and establishes the melody before the chorus or bridge.
Chorus – The main melody or refrain of a musical composition. Not all songs use a chorus. Our example does not use a chorus.
Bridge – A separate melody, usually providing melodic relief from a series of verses.
Turnaround – A group of chords, at the end of a verse or song, that takes the arrangement back to the beginning.
Ending – A section of the composition that brings the song to a close.
Repeat Signs Indicates a section is to be repeated from the sign to the sign.
First & Second Endings Play first ending, go back to beginning or repeat sign and repeat section. At end of section, bypass first ending and play second ending.
Coda Signs – *D.S. al Coda (dal segno)* "from the sign" indicates that a section of a composition is to be repeated beginning at the sign 𝄋 and continuing until the sign ⊕ or *Fine*, or end.

STUDY EXERCISE 〔61〕 *SWING BALLAD TEMPO 114*

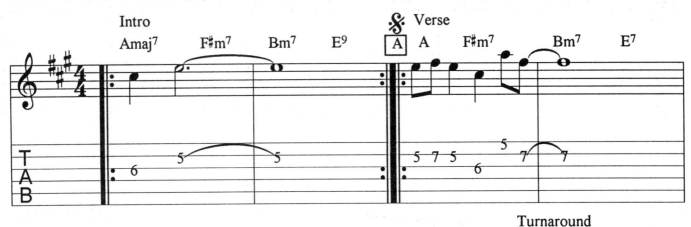

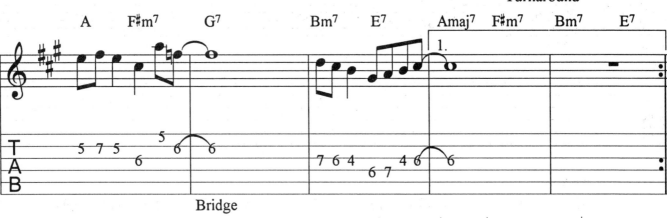

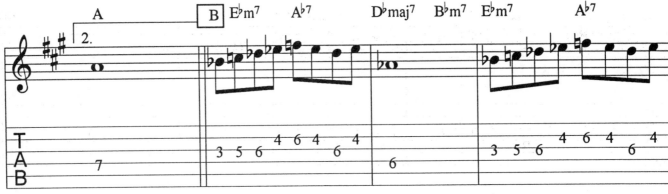

< 117 >

STUDY EXERCISE 61

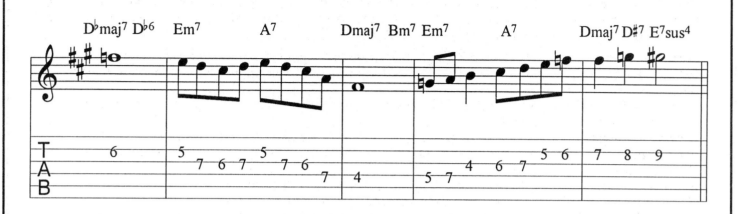

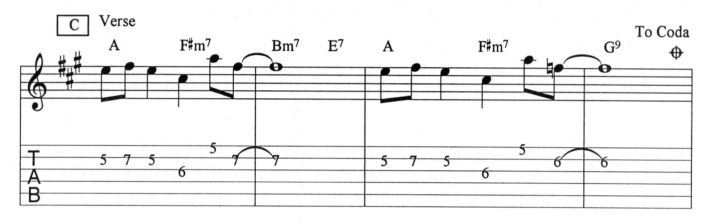

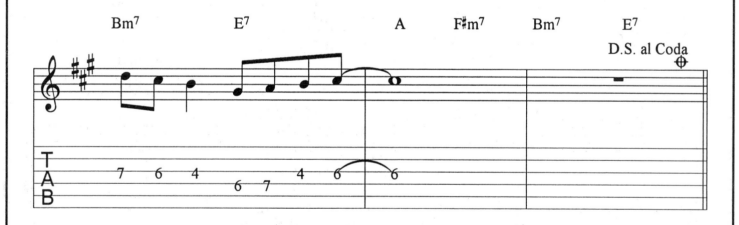

TRIADIC IMPROVISATION

section five REVIEW

─── STREET SMARTS ───

Always look for the ii-V-I chord group. It will identify the proper scale to play at that point in the song.

─── PAGE 109 ───

─── STREET SMARTS ───

When all chords are common to a sub-chord group, we may utilize triadic harmonization to play through the scales they share in common.

─── PAGE 111 ───

< 119 >

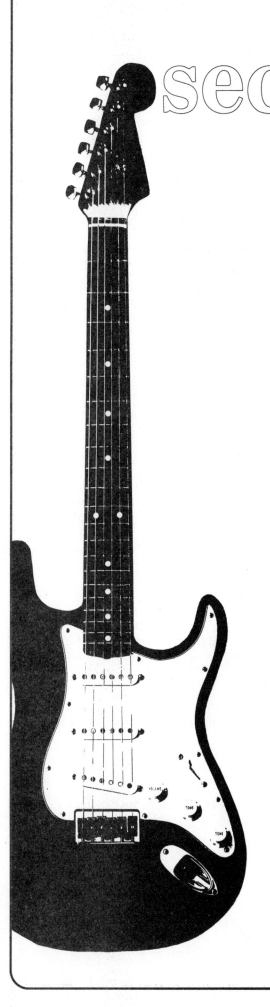

section six

TOOLS OF CREATIVE IMPROVISATION

Knowledge of scales alone will not allow you to create exciting or even enjoyable music. You must learn the creative tools required to transform simple note patterns into exciting solos. In this section, we will explore the *tricks* of creative playing.

FOUR STEPS ESSENTIAL FOR SUCCESS

1. Definiteness of Purpose. *Know what you want to accomplish. Set goals and constantly monitor your progress.*

2. Desire. *It is comparatively easy to acquire and maintain persistence in pursuing your goals, if you maintain a burning desire for their accomplishment.*

3. Self-Reliance. *Believe in yourself and your plan of action. March forward in small steps, for this allows you to overcome setbacks, and not lose faith in yourself or your plan.*

4. Accurate Knowledge. *Knowing one's plan is sound, based on experience or observation, encourages persistence and helps to overcome the effects of negative events that are bound to interfere with your plans.*

CREATIVE TOOLS

HAMMER-ON (Measure 6)

A "hammer-on" is a way of raising the pitch of a note without striking the string twice. A hammer-on is accomplished by picking the first note, and while holding it down, striking the string sharply with another finger at the proper fret required to sound the higher note. The second note is not picked; the impact of the finger striking the string will create the sound of the hammered-on tone. The string must be struck firmly and close to the correct fret.

PULL-OFF (Measure 2, 8)

A "pull-off" is a device that allows you to lower the pitch of a note without striking the string a second time to create the second, lower tone. To create a pull-off, place a finger on both the higher fretted note and the fret of the lower note. Strike the string and without picking the string again, pull the finger off of the higher fret sharply enough to create the tone of the lower note.

HAMMER-ON / PULL-OFF (Measure 2, 7)

A hammer-on/pull-off is a device that combines both effects to produce a series of notes in rapid succession without the need to pick each individual note.

STRING BEND (Measure 2)

A string bend, commonly referred to as a "bend", is a device that allows you to raise the pitch of a note by pushing a fretted string sideways, increasing the string tension. Example: pushing the second string sideways, up toward the third string. The string may be pushed (bent), sufficiently to raise the pitch of a fretted note a half step, a half bend (A to A#), or a full bend, one full step (A to B). A bend allows you to raise a note's pitch smoothly, creating a unique tonal shift.

BEND AND RELEASE (Measure 14)

A "bend and release" raises and lowers the pitch of a note. This is accomplished by firmly fretting the string and pushing the string up to create the desired pitch; then, while keeping full pressure on the string, allowing it to return to its original state.

VIBRATO (Last Measure)

A "vibrato" is created by striking the string and rapidly bending and releasing a fretted note with a rapid, left-hand movement. (A shaking movement.)

SLIDE (Measure 3)

A "slide" is a way of moving a fretted note to another pitch. A note is sounded, and with the finger firmly on the string, we slide the finger up or down to a new location on the fingerboard.

> ┌─ **PRACTICE TIP** ──────────────
> We recommend that you go back over previous examples and use these creative tools to create your own unique solos. This is most effective when playing along with the Audio Companion.

STUDY EXERCISE  62

ROCK & ROLL TEMPO 120

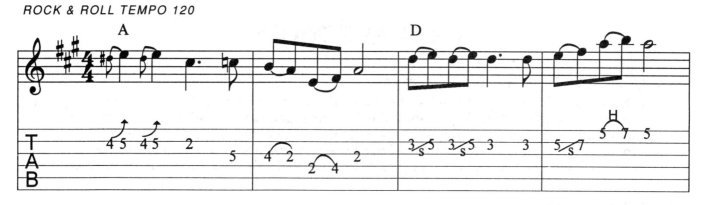

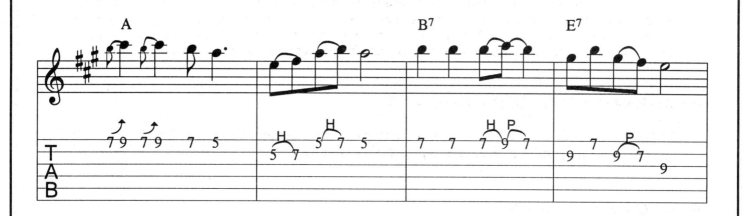

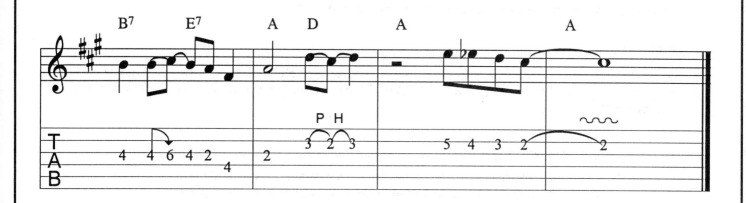

< 122 >

PHRASING

SOLOS

Solos are not disjointed, rambling attempts to showcase a repertoire of "licks". Solos should always be appropriate to the song. Solos make musical statements call "motifs, rifts or fills". In creating effective solos, it is important to not allow the melodic flow to be interrupted by chord changes or key center changes. Once we have made a melodic statement, it is desirable to refine and develop the idea fully before moving on to another idea or statement. Think of it as completing a thought in conversation before moving on to another subject. The real art of improvisation lies in the ability to play an effective solo over the rhythmic character of the song, creating new phrases that compliment and build upon previous ideas.

"Motifs" are like short sentences or an expression of thought. They are usually three or four notes in length and used to make an "identifiable" musical statement within the solo. They are often used in repetition throughout a solo, to create the "theme" of the piece, or the identifiable musical statement of which the listener comes to identify. Motifs are created from scales and arpeggios, and shaped by expression tools (bends, slides or hammer-ons). The Street Smarts word for motifs is "lick". Develop the "ear" to hear motifs in songs, since they shape the guitarist's playing style.

A short statement is called a motif – a longer statement is called a "riff". A riff may be two, four or eight measures long. Often it is comprised of short motifs connected together to create a longer solo line. Riffs are often called the "hook" lines, or a statement the listener comes to identify as the main theme of the song. The riff of a song can appear at the beginning of a song and may reoccur as the arranger desires.

Study Exercise 63 has been arranged to allow you to practice creating "fills", measures where our lead guitar steps out, providing you the opportunity to improvise using motifs and riffs of your creation. A soloist should always build upon the established theme. Therefore, your fills should maintain the integrity of what has already been played. Develop the ability to articulate and refine your solos so you may play "on the fly", without forethought. Use your creativeness – play and have fun!

PRACTICE TIP

Go back and play previous examples and study the phrasing. See if you can identify the motifs and riffs. This is especially useful if you have the Audio Companion.

STUDY EXERCISE 63

COUNTRY TEMPO 85

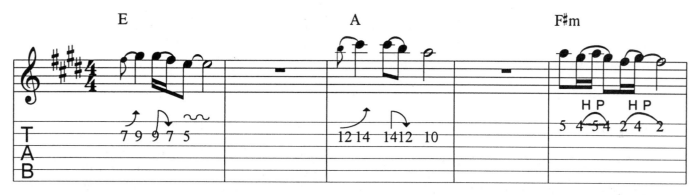

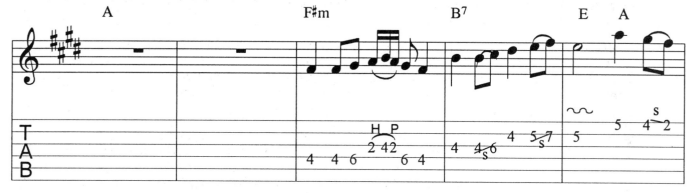

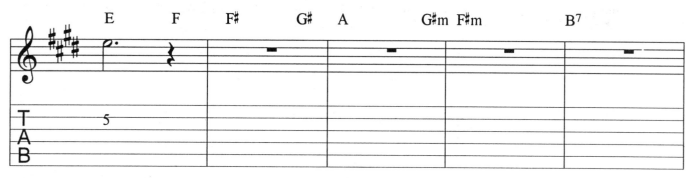

TOOLS OF CREATIVE IMPROVISATION

EAR TRAINING

Most beginners have a great deal of trouble following a piece of music with their ear, so when the ability to hear the tonality of the melody and rhythm has not been developed, it is almost impossible to improvise solos.

We must "hear" the chords, and have the "ear" to follow chord changes because improvisation is based on playing a scale pattern that will harmonize the chord progression within a song. No matter how many scale patterns we know, or how fast we can play "licks", if we play the wrong scale over a given chord progression, we create "bad" music.

A book, in itself, is mute. It can convey information; however, the reader cannot hear the music. And after all, we purchase a book and study the information contained therein so we may create music on our instrument. But, without a trained ear, how do we know if what we play is correct?

SENSE OF RHYTHM

A developed sense of rhythm is as important as ear training in creating successful solos. Rhythm sets the tempo, creates the rhythmic phrases and establishes the texture of the song. A Latin piece sounds quite different from a Rock or Country song. Listen to the drum beat, bass line, and the rhythm guitar chords, and you will find that is these elements of the song that the lead guitarists is playing against.

As with ear training, it is most difficult to study a book and learn to play proper phrases that fit within the structure set up by the rhythm instruments. It is for this reason, we feel the Audio Companion is so important to the beginner. Not only do we demonstrate the technical information, we provide you with your own band with which to practice. We lead you through many types of songs and rhythms and explain how to develop your ability to improvise interesting and correctly played solos.

SUCCESS STEPS

1. What Key is the song played? Is it Major or Minor? (Key Signature)

2. What is the chord progression?

3. What is the rhythmic structure of the song? (Time Signature)

3. What is the proper scale(s) that can be used?

4. What is the most appropriate scale pattern(s)?

5. Where are the scale runs and arpeggios located?

6. What playing techniques are appropriate (bend, hammer-ons, etc.)?

TIME SIGNATURES

We have, in our written examples, utilized many types of rhythms to help familiarize you with a wide verity of music, for music is divided into many styles, each with its own unique rhythmic 'feel' of which the guitarists must be aware when creating solos. Below, we present for your study, five of the more common time signatures, and indicate an example where it has been used in our study exercises.

Country- Straight Feel   Adjust tempo to taste

Rock & Roll- Double Time Feel   Adjust tempo to taste

Country- Double Time Feel

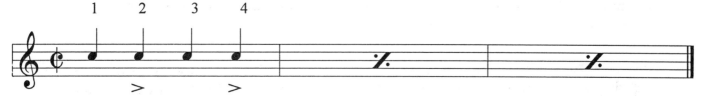

Shuffle- Triple Time Feel   Adjust tempo to Taste

Swing-Bee Bop- Triple Time Feel

Bee   Bop-ah   Bee   Bop-ah

<126>

ROCK SONG

If you have thoughtfully studied, assimilated and practiced the information we have presented in this book, you should be ready to try your hand at improvising solos with a band. The following four songs give you the opportunity to create your own melodies, licks and riffs. We recommend you record the rhythm pattern, or have a friend play the chords so you can put into practice the art of actually playing scales over chords!

The audio Companion – It is at this point in your education we feel you would benefit most from this exciting innovation . . . the opportunity to practice with your own band! If you have the Audio Companion, listen to the four, full-arranged songs, each with its own sound and style and make notes – where are the repeats and turn-arounds? Where are the key centers? What is the most appropriate scale or mode to play over each sub-chord group?

ROCK & ROLL SONG

The first tune is a Rock & Roll song. It should be played at a moderate rock & roll beat. The chords are in the key of *A* major.

ROCK SONG

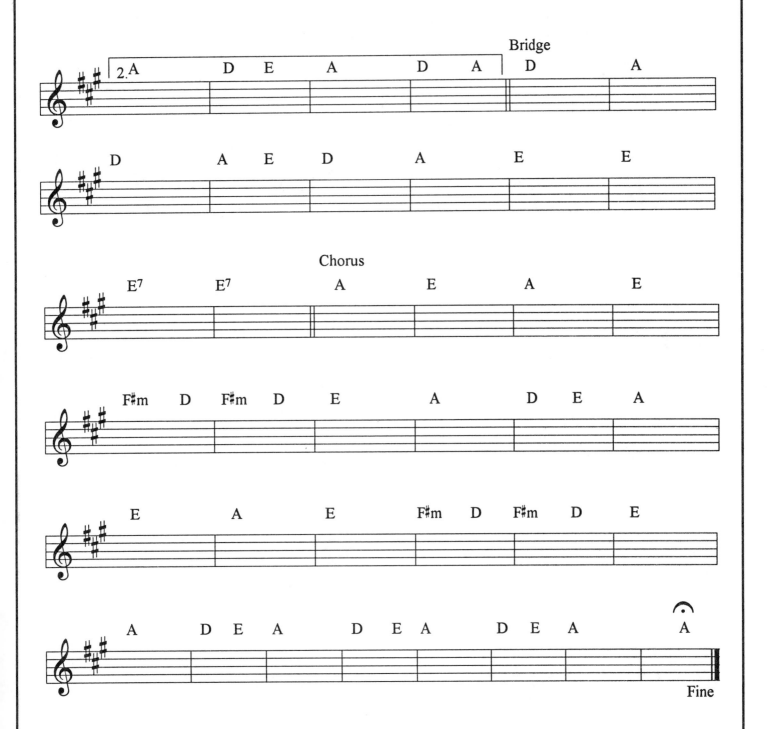

<128>

COUNTRY SONG

COUNTRY SONG

This should be played with a country two-step beat, medium tempo. This song has all the components of arrangement, so it is a long song and you will have a great time developing your own melodies for the verse, bridge and chorus. The more you play the song, the more creative things you will come up with. All chords are in the key of *G* major, so use the *G* major scale.

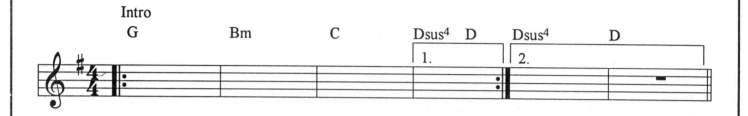

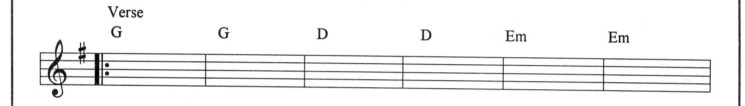

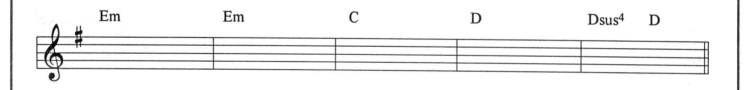

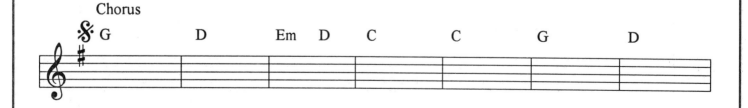

<129>

COUNTRY SONG

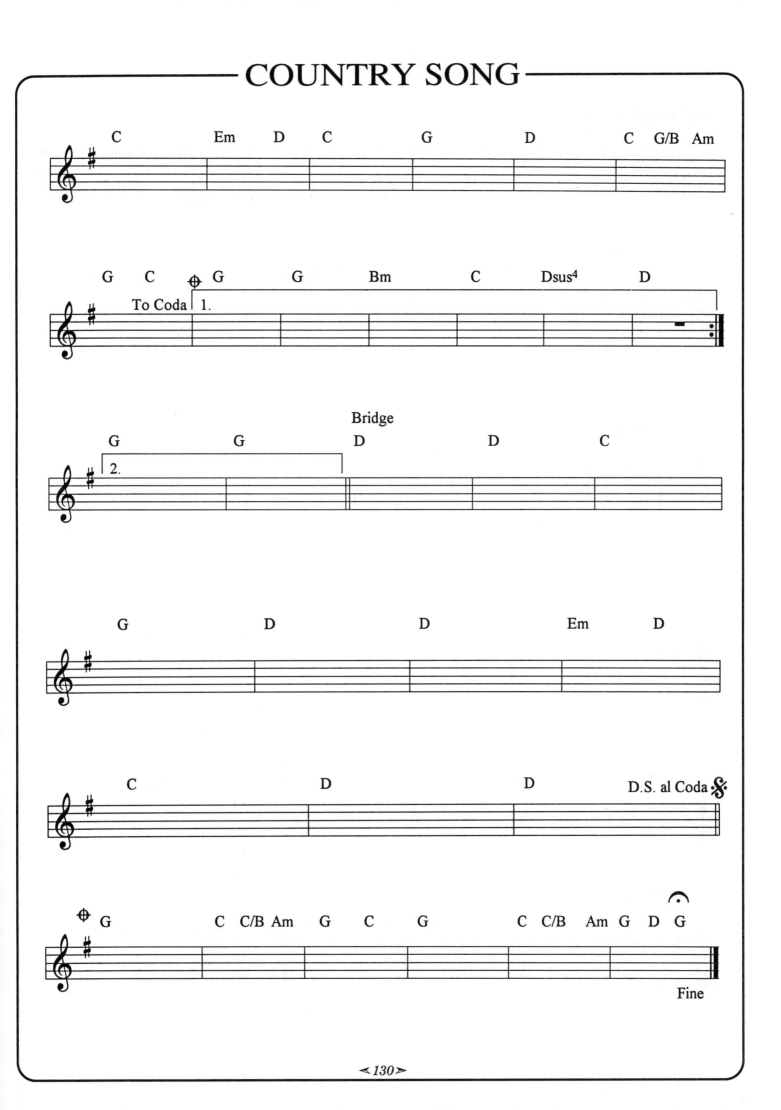

< 130 >

BLUES SONG

BLUES SONG

This song should be played with a shuffle beat. The tempo is up to you. The Mixolydian and Dorian modes work well in creating blues solos.

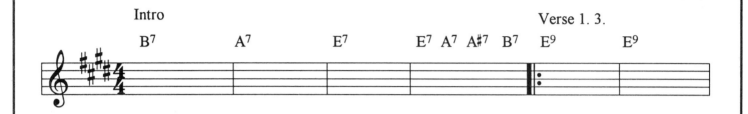

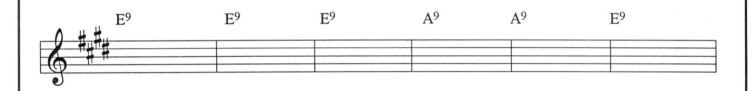

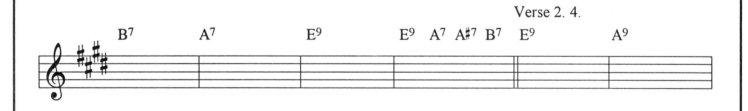

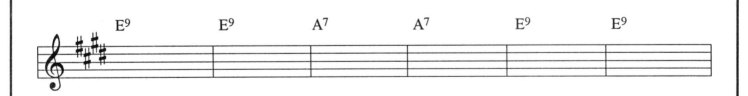

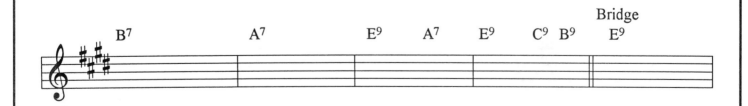

BLUES SONG

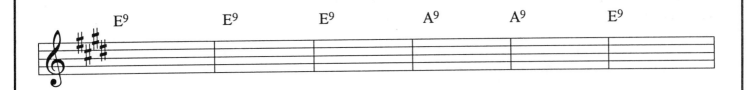

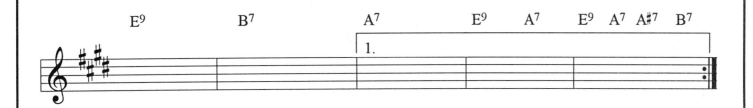

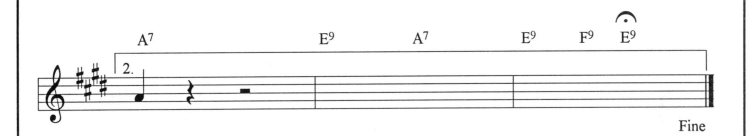

Fine

JAZZ SONG

JAZZ SONG

Do not expect to get this one very quickly, for it is the most difficult of the four arrangements. It should be played as a jazz swing, and you can use your own tempo. If you encounter points in the song with which you are unfamiliar, use your head and think your way through, applying the knowledge of triadic harmonization presented in this book.

JAZZ SONG

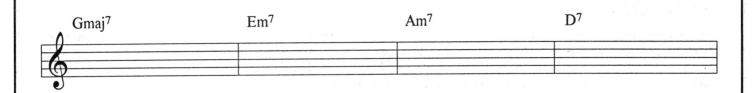

Gmaj⁷   Em⁷   Am⁷   D⁷

Verse

Dm⁷   G¹³   Cmaj⁷   C♯dim   Dm⁷

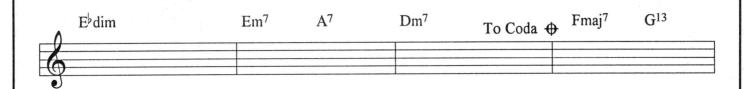

E♭dim   Em⁷   A⁷   Dm⁷   To Coda ⊕   Fmaj⁷   G¹³

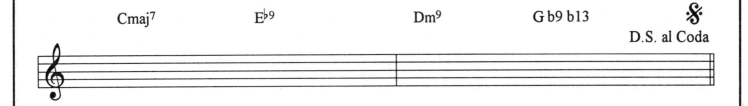

Cmaj⁷   E♭9   Dm⁹   G b9 b13   𝄋

D.S. al Coda

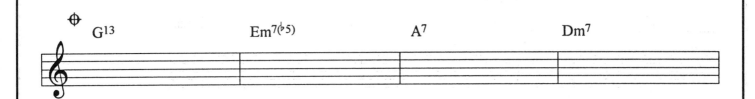

⊕   G¹³   Em⁷⁽♭5⁾   A⁷   Dm⁷

Ending tag

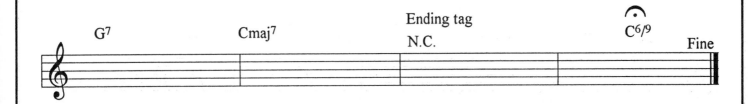

G⁷   Cmaj⁷   N.C.   C⁶ᐟ⁹   Fine

CHORD DIAGRAMS

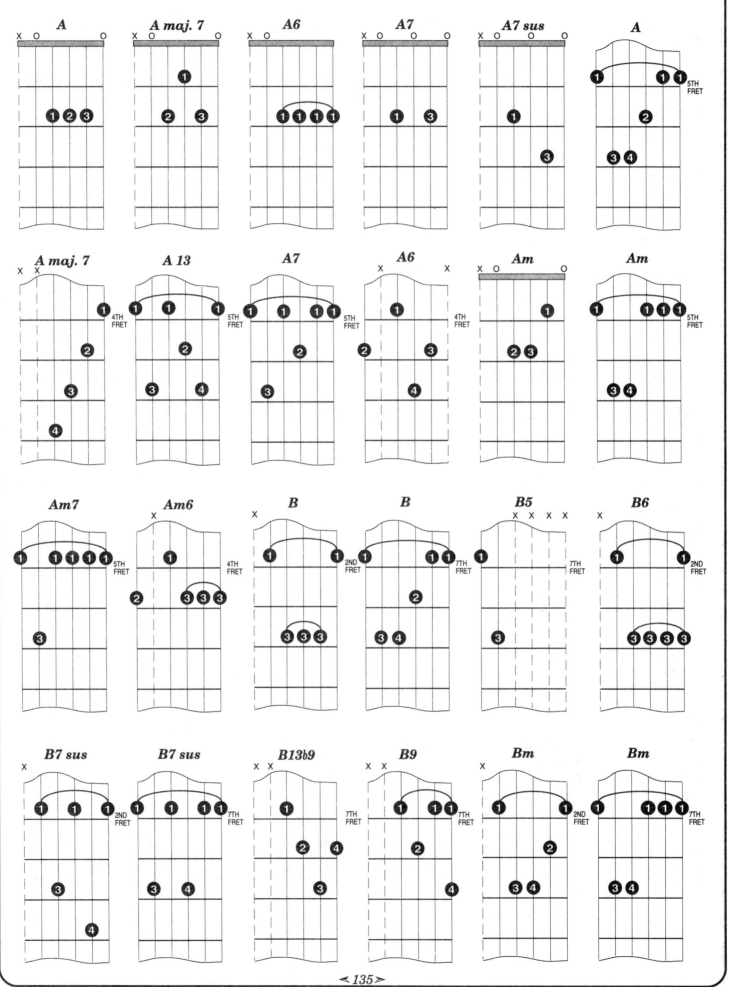

< 135 >

CHORD DIAGRAMS

Bm7   Bm7   Bm7b5   Bbm7   Bb9   C

Cmaj.7   C6   C7   C add 9   C9   C dim.

C Aug   C⁶/₉   C maj.9   C maj.7   C maj.7   C

C   C#m   C#m   C#m7b5   C#m7   C#7

< 136 >

CHORD DIAGRAMS

C#5

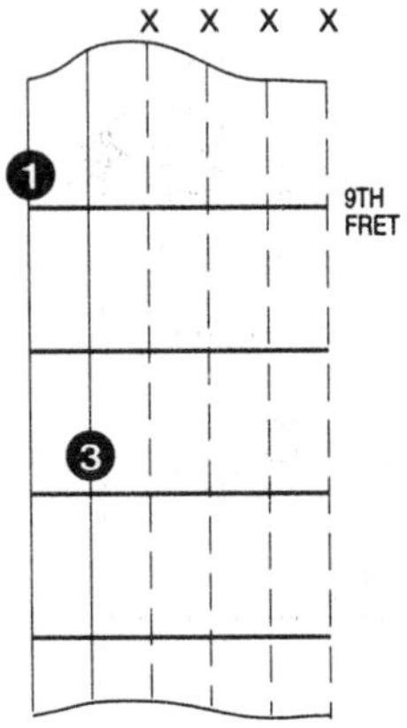

C#m9

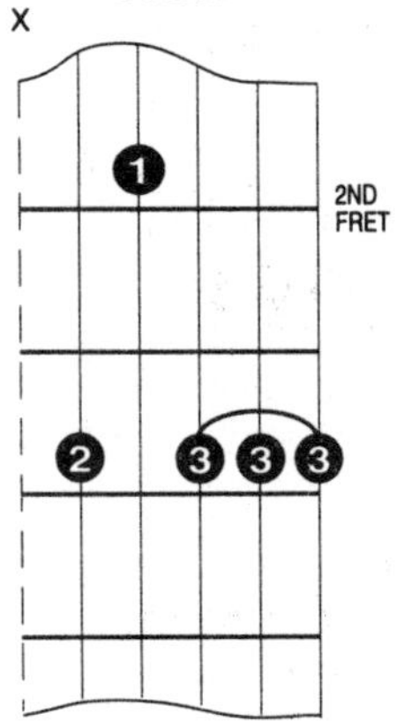

C#

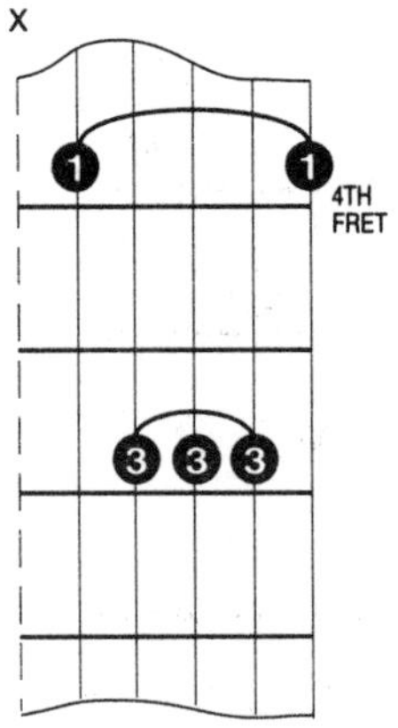

D

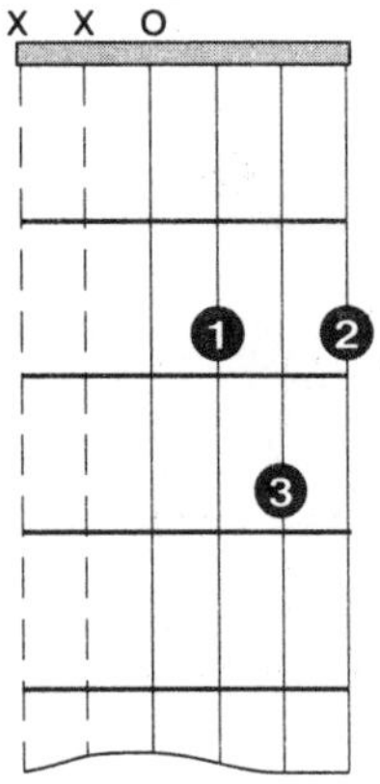

D

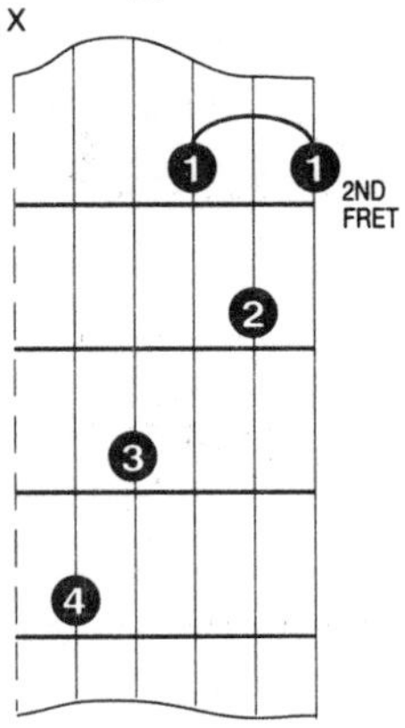

D

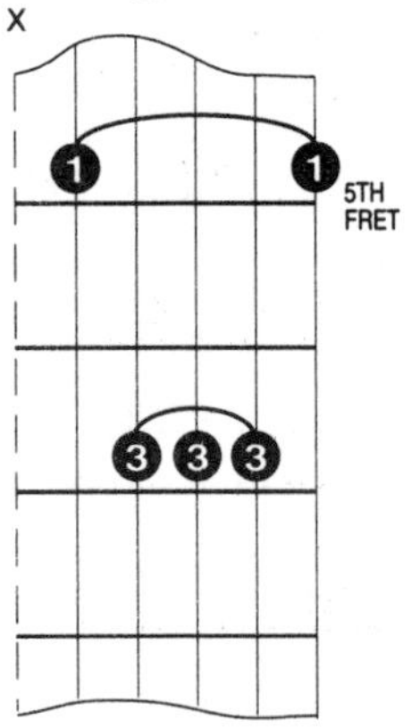

D maj.7

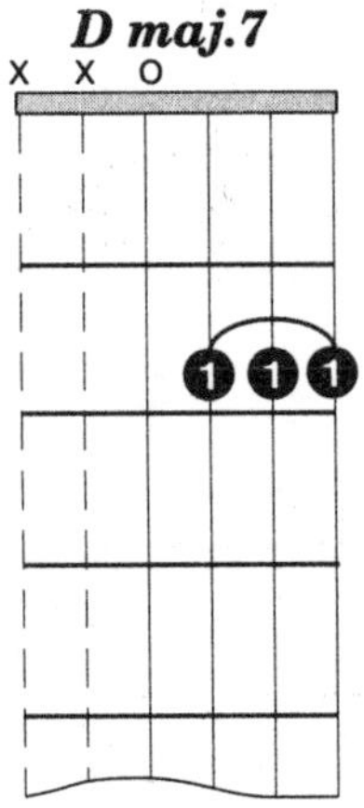

D maj.7

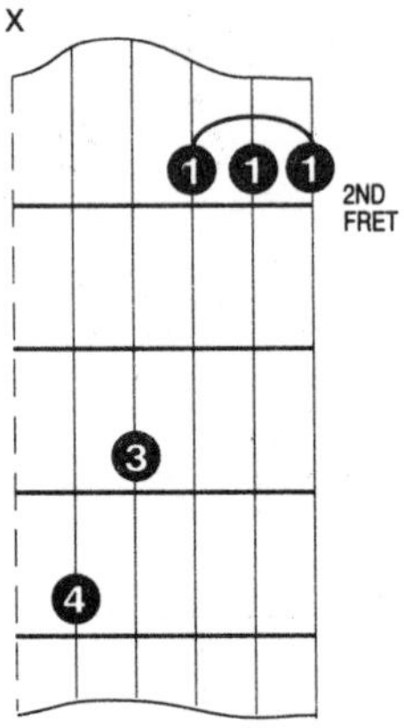

D maj.7

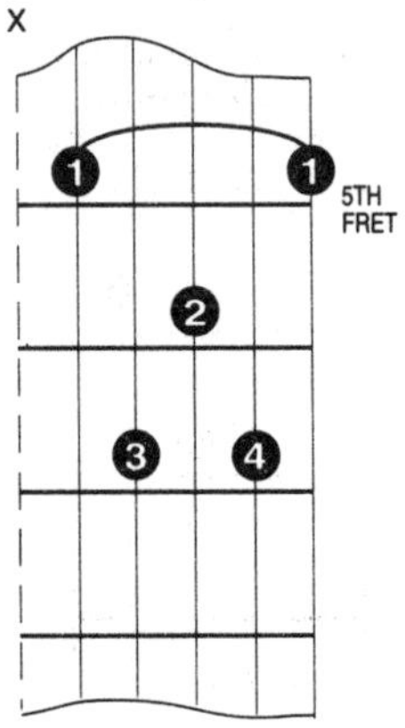

D7

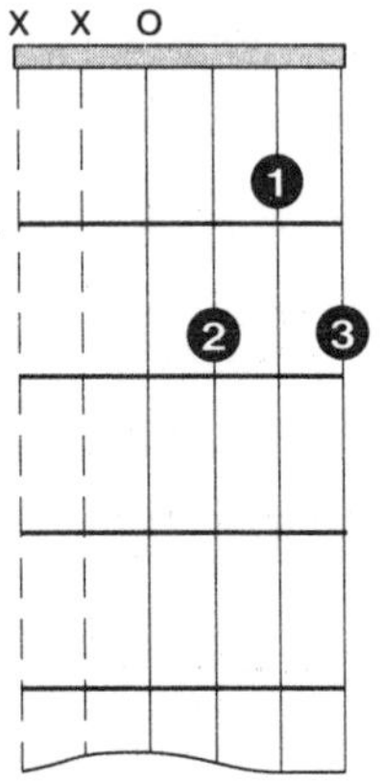

D7

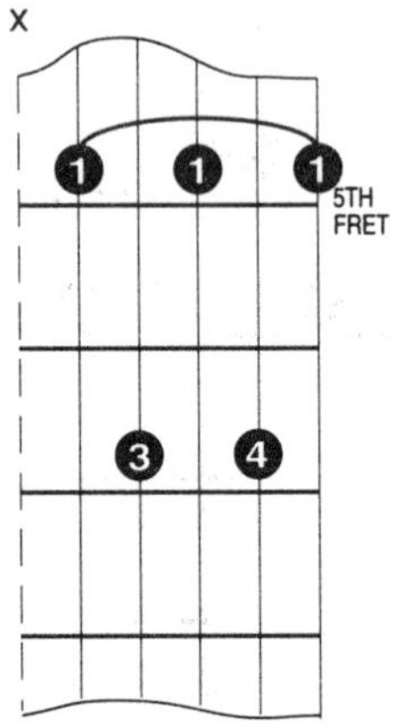

C/D

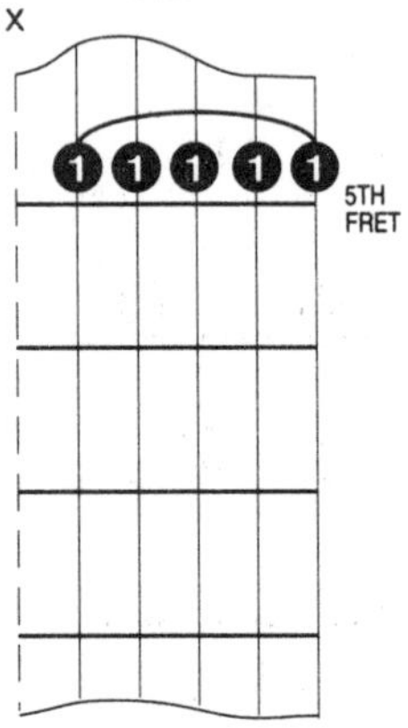

D9

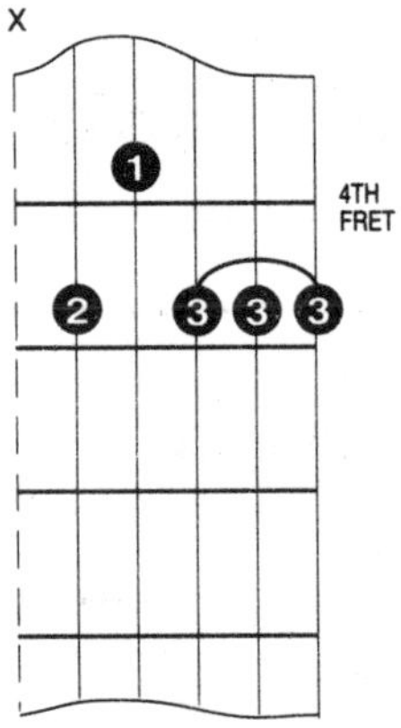

D7 sus

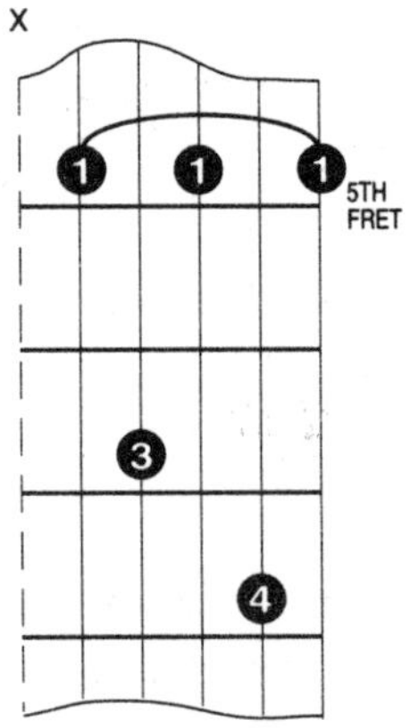

D7b9

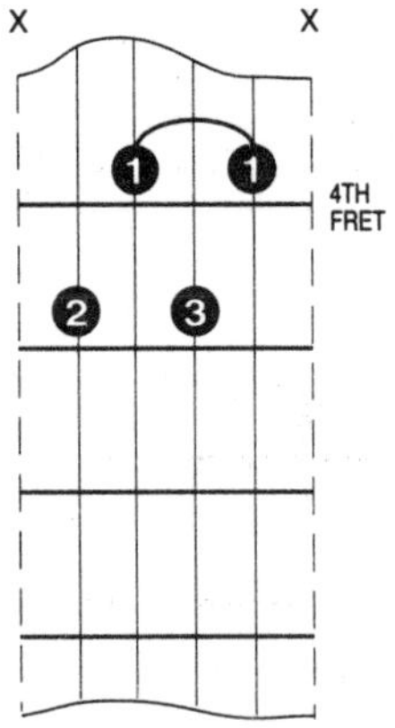

D6

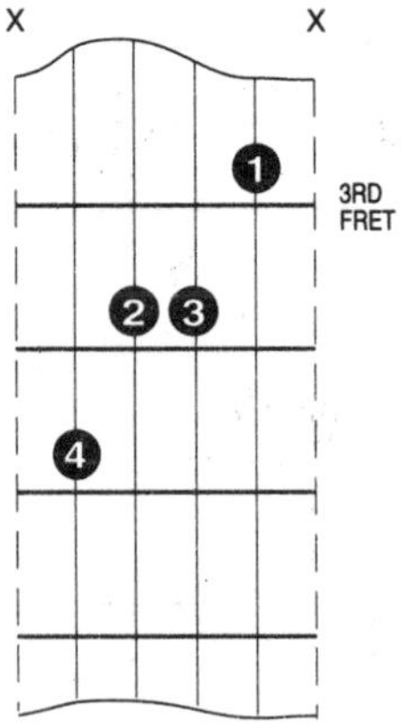

Db maj.7

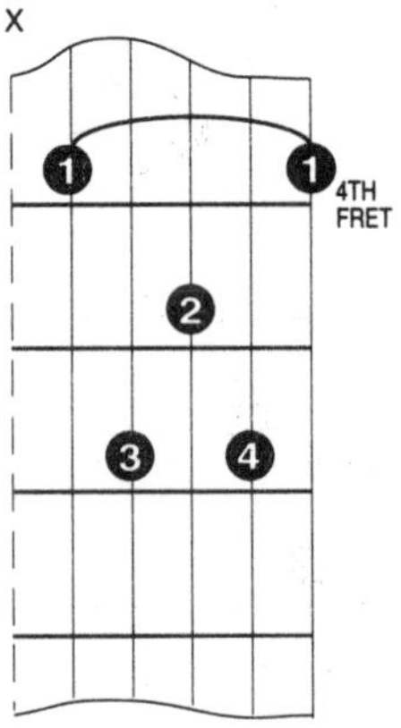

D#7

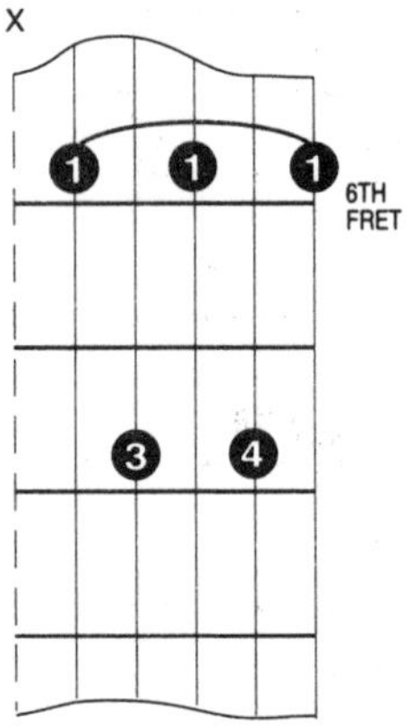

Dm

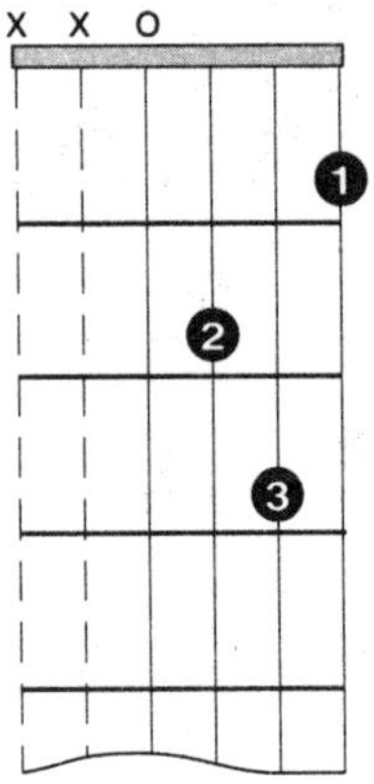

Dm

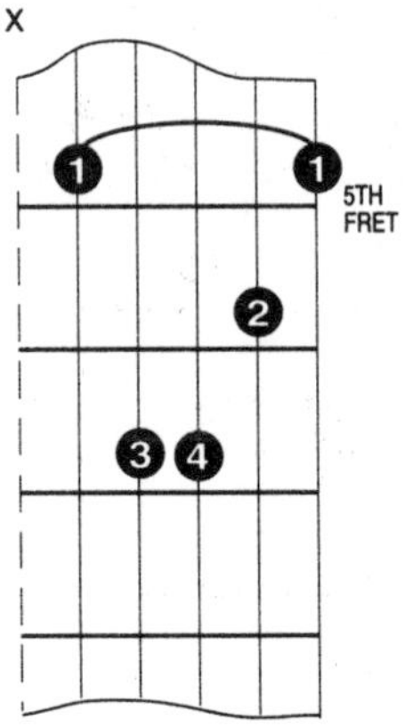

Dm7

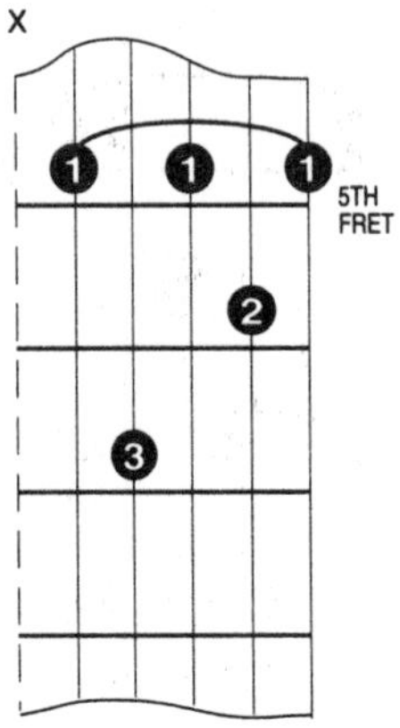

D#m7b5

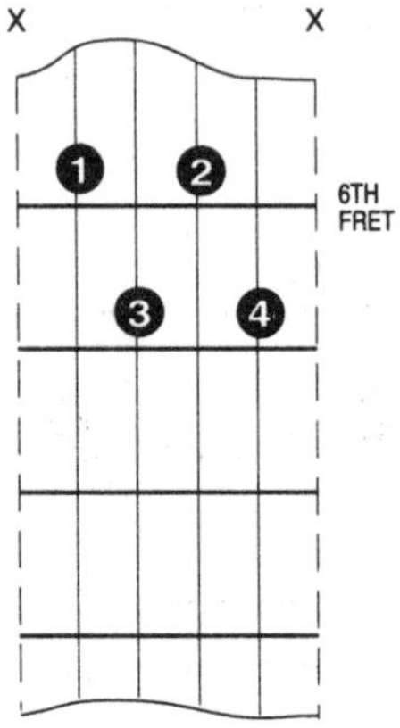

D#°

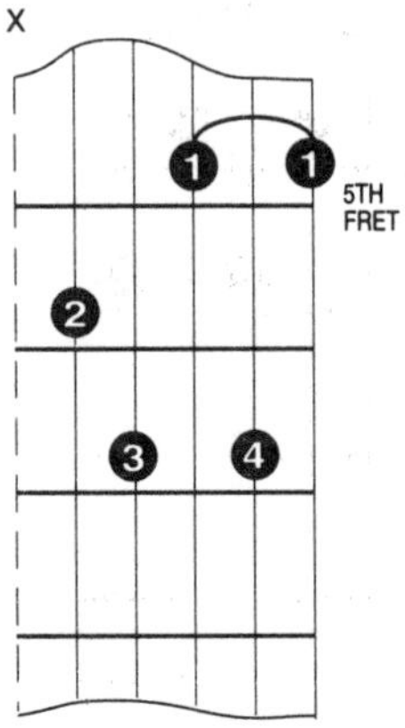

E

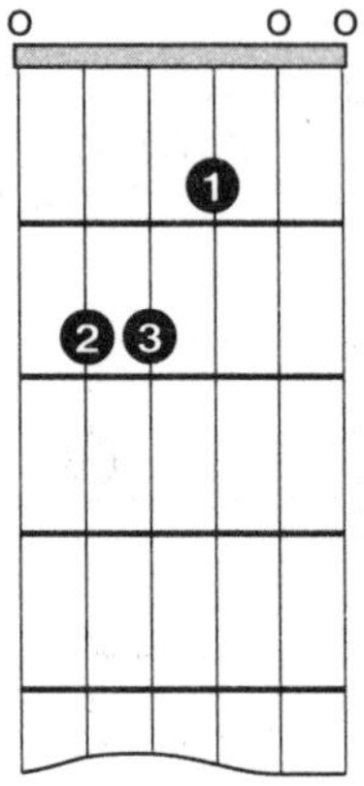

CHORD DIAGRAMS

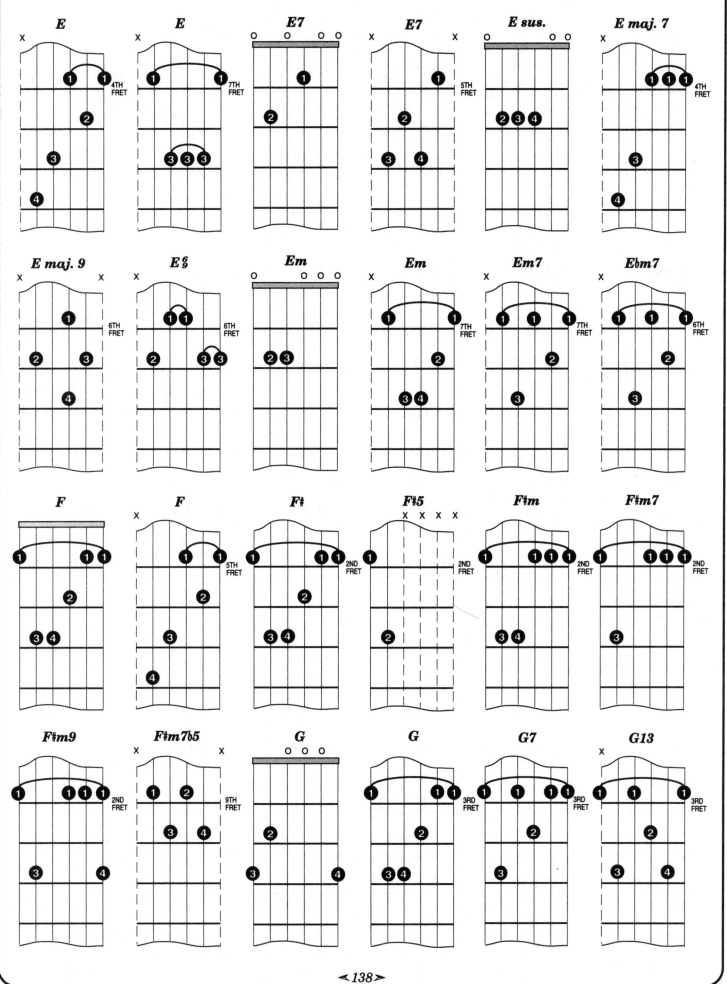

CHORD DIAGRAMS

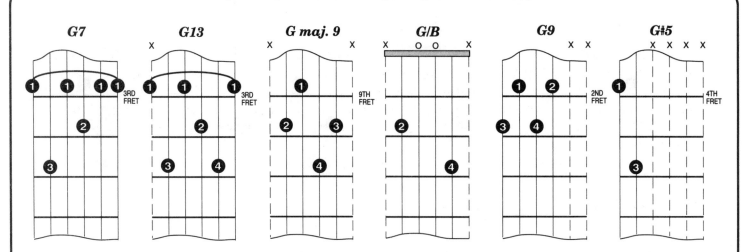

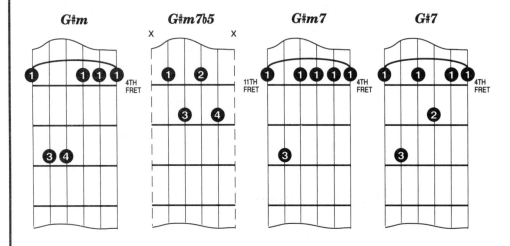

RULES OF MODAL HARMONY

With at least three scale possibilities to play over each chord, is there one that may be more appropriate to use? While we can play scales from any note of a chords triad, you will find that each scale will cause a shift in tonality and the scale you choose may not reflect the tonal intent of the song. It is generally more appropriate to play a scale (mode) from the root note of the chord, the Tonic note (1). This will normally conform to the established rules of modal harmony.

IONIAN MODE *1st degree*
Tonal characteristic: Major

The Ionian mode is the Major Scale and can always be played over major chords. The Major Pentonic scale is a derivative of the Ionian mode.

DORIAN MODE *2nd degree*
Tonal characteristic: Minor

The Dorian mode is used over the ii-V chord change. It is a preferred scale in "Blues" songs.

PHRYGIAN MODE *3rd degree*
Tonal characteristic: Minor or Major

The Phrygian mode is the most commonly played over minor chords.

LYDIAN MODE *4th degree*
Tonal characteristic: Major

The Lydian mode is a preferred scale to play over major chords.

MIXOLYDIAN *5th degree*
Tonal characteristic: Major

The Mixolydian mode is often called the Dominant Scale, because it harmonizes the Dominant Seventh Chord, and can generally be played over the V7 chord, and its extended note: 9th, 11th and 13th.

AEOLIAN MODE *6th degree*
Tonal characteristic: Minor

The Aeolian mode is the Natural Minor Scale, also referred to as the Relative Minor Scale, and may always be played over minor chords. The Aeolian mode, is also called the "Pure" Minor Scale. The Minor Pentatonic Scale is a derivative of the Aeolian mode.

LOCRIAN MODE *7th degree*
Tonal characteristic: Diminished/Minor

The Locrian mode is, because of its tonality, the mode of choice to play over the ii minor chord. The diminished characteristic allows the Locrian mode to be played over the V7 chord.

TRIAD HARMONIZATION CHART

KEY OF *C* MAJOR

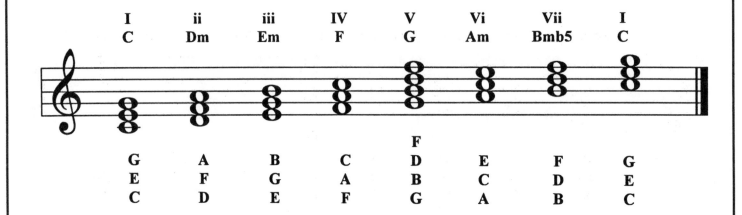

I	ii	iii	IV	V	Vi	Vii	I
C	Dm	Em	F	G	Am	Bmb5	C

				F			
G	A	B	C	D	E	F	G
E	F	G	A	B	C	D	E
C	D	E	F	G	A	B	C

KEY OF G MAJOR

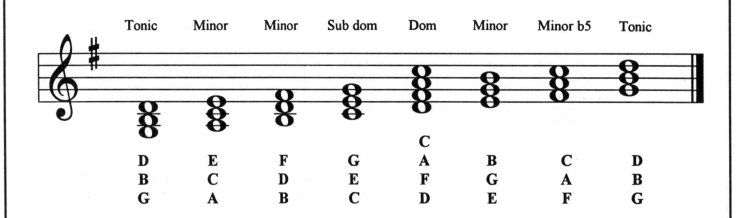

Tonic	Minor	Minor	Sub dom	Dom	Minor	Minor b5	Tonic

				C			
D	E	F	G	A	B	C	D
B	C	D	E	F	G	A	B
G	A	B	C	D	E	F	G

TRIAD HARMONIZATION CHART

KEY OF D MAJOR

Tonic	Minor	Minor	Sub dom	Dom	Minor	Minor b5	Tonic
				G			
A	B	C#	D	E	F#	G	A
F#	G	A	B	C	D	E	F#
D	E	F#	G	A	B	C	D

KEY OF A MAJOR

Tonic	Minor	Minor	Sub dom	Dom	Minor	Minor b5	Tonic
				D			
E	F#	G#	A	B	C#	F	E
C#	D	E	F#	G#	A	Bb	C#
A	B	C#	D	E	F#	G	A

TRIAD HARMONIZATION CHART

KEY OF *E* MAJOR

	Tonic	Minor	Minor	Sub dom	Dom	Minor	Minor b5	Tonic
					A			
	B	C#	D#	E	F#	G#	B	B
	G#	A	B	C#	D#	E	G#	G#
	E	F#	G#	A	B	C#	F	E

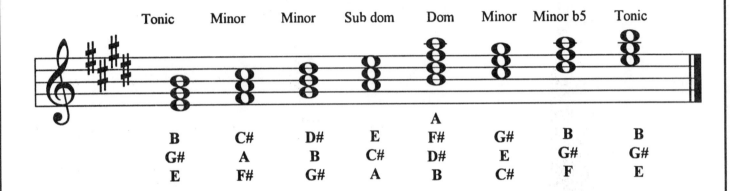

KEY OF *F* MAJOR

	Tonic	Minor	Minor	Sub dom	Dom	Minor	Minor b5	Tonic
					Bb			
	C	D	E	F	G	A	Bb	C
	A	Bb	C	Db	E	F	G	A
	F	G	A	Bb	C	D	E	F

TEACHER HELPERS

BLANK CHORD DIAGRAMS

BLANK STAFF SHEETS

NOTE PAGES

TEACHER SECTION

The art of improvisation is a vast, complex subject, and one that certainly goes well beyond the scope of this book. By necessity, we have touched upon many worthwhile ideas; ideas we hope you will pursue on your own. We do believe the information we have presented will require many hours of thoughtful study, but with the aid of the Audio Companion, many hours of enjoyable practice time as well.

"Scales Over Chords" brings together a lifetime of knowledge that may be taught to students at all levels of development. If, as a teacher, you find the material and ideas this book helpful, we encourage you to incorporate them into your teaching program and create exercises customized for the individual student.

As teachers, the authors know the value of "good" educational books and their scarcity. It is with this thought in mind, we include blank charts and staff sheets in this section. As a student, use them to save your creative ideas as you develop your improvisational skills.

The Audio Companion is also an invaluable instructional aid and was developed to not only demonstrate the written examples, but to also provide teachers with a valuable teaching tool that will bring the excitement of "live" music to weekly lesson and practice sessions.

< 145 >

CHORD DIAGRAMS

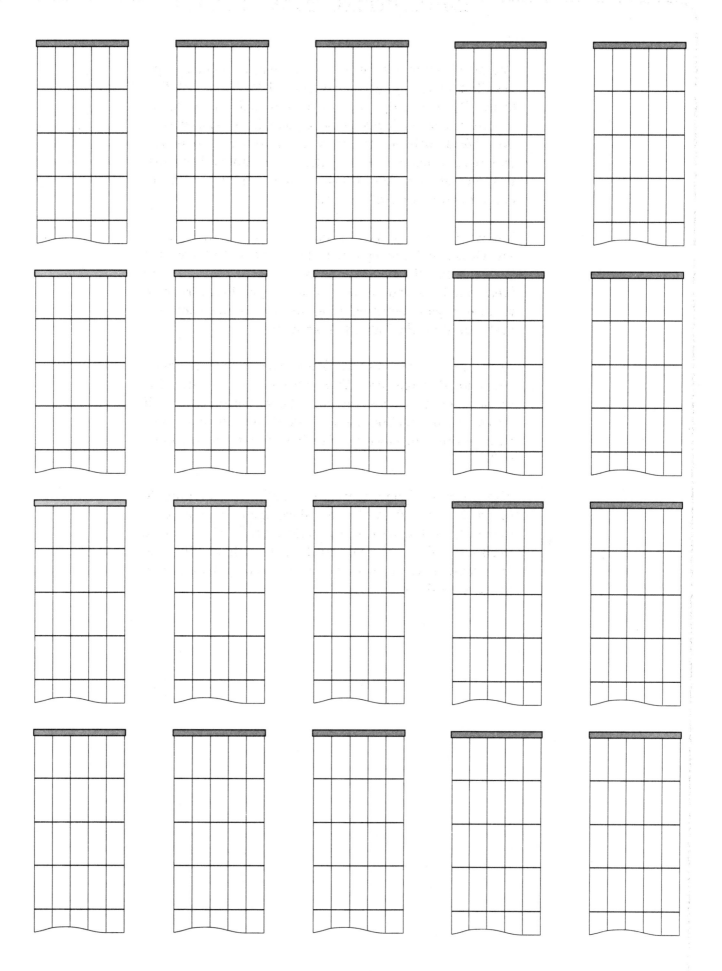

CHORD DIAGRAMS

CHORD DIAGRAMS

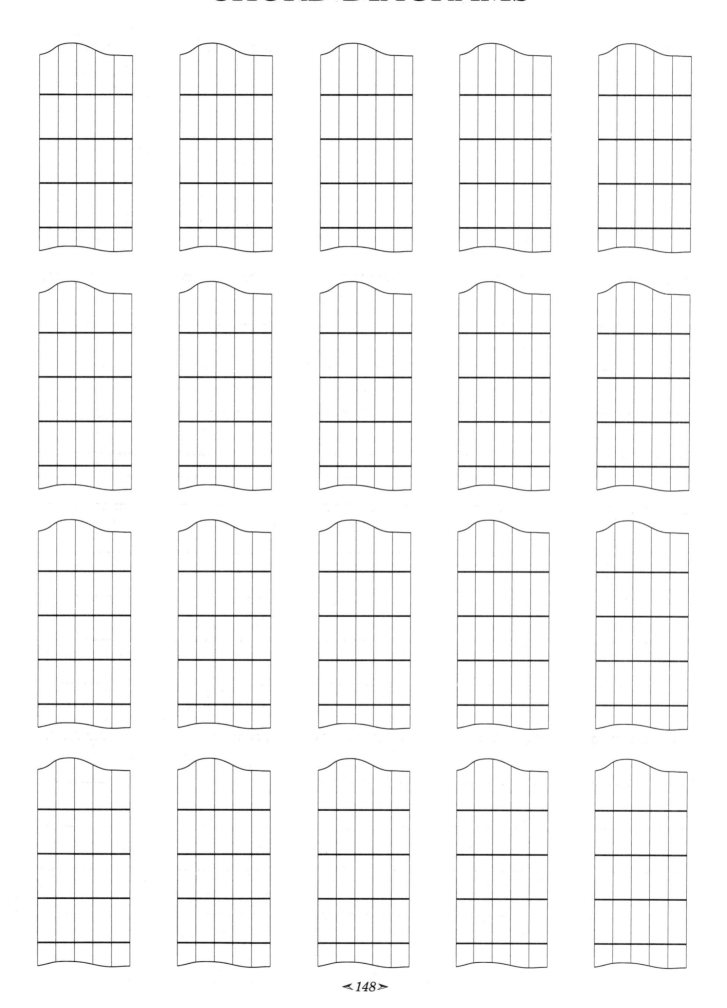

CHORD DIAGRAMS

TWO MEASURE STAFF SHEET

TWO MEASURE STAFF SHEET

TWO MEASURE STAFF SHEET

FOUR MEASURE STAFF SHEET

FOUR MEASURE STAFF SHEET

FIVE MEASURE STAFF SHEET

<155>

FIVE MEASURE STAFF SHEET

NOTES • NOTES • NOTES

NOTES • NOTES • NOTES

< 158 >

NOTES • NOTES • NOTES

SCALES OVER CHORDS

How to improvise . . . and never play bad notes!

Audio Companion

Book design, layout and music engraving by
WILBUR M. SAVIDGE
Music production by
RANDY LEE VRADENBURG
Editing engineer
SCOTT LOEHR
Recorded at
BIG TIME AUDIO, Dallas, TX
Mixed and edited at
FOLK LOEHR PRODUCTIONS

Musicians:

RANDY LEE VRADENBURG – lead guitar
REX JOHNSON – bass guitar
BOBBY BREAUX – drums
ANDY MICHLIN – piano
JEFF BAIR – sax
SCOTT LEOHR – keyboard
JOHN WALDEN – fiddle

The "audio companion" is designed to (1) audibly demonstrate the written examples in the book *"Scales Over Chords: How to improvise and never play bad notes"*, and (2) to provide you with your own band with which you may practice solo improvisation. We also include the rhythm chords used in our examples so you may practice playing rhythm. You must know how to improvise to make the most of the Audio Companion, for it is not the subject of this booklet to explain this complex subject. If you lack the skills of improvisation, we suggest you obtain a copy of the companion book *"Scales Over Chords"*. In this comprehensive text, we present the rules of improvisation in a concise, straightforward way that, with the Audio Companion, makes learning improvisation fun and exciting!

— *Wilbur M. Savidge*

How to use the Audio Companion

The Audio Companion presents the chord charts and play-along "Jam Tracks" to 66 songs played in a variety of musical styles and tempos. Excluding the last four songs, all examples are recorded with the band on the left channel and our lead guitar on the right channel. Your stereo's balance control may be used to eliminate our lead guitar so you may practice improvisational solos, or cut the band and practice playing rhythm. PAN LEFT to cut the lead guitar for soloing . . . PAN RIGHT to cut the band for rhythm practice. Set the balance control in the center position to hear the songs in stereo. The last four examples are full arrangements, giving you the opportunity to follow a studio chart and play lead with a Country, Rock, Blues and Jazz band.

PLAY ALONG JamTracks

Study Exercise   12   Bossanova Tempo 132

D   Em   F#m G   A   Bm   C#m7(♭5) D   Em   A   Em   A   G   A Em A D

Study Exercise   13   Rock & Roll Tempo 129

Dm   C   Bm7(♭5) C   G   F   Dm   F   Bm7(♭5)   Am Dm G   C

Study Exercise   14   6/8 Feel Tempo 78

A   D   E   A   F#m   Bm   E   A

Study Exercise   15   Rap Tempo 113

G   Bm   C   D7   Am   D7   G   Em   C   Bm   Am   C   D7   G

Study Exercise   16   Country Tempo 111

E   E   A   A   B   B   E   E

Study Exercise   18   Arpeggios

D   Em   F#m G   A   Bm C#m7(♭5) D C#m7(♭5) B#m A   G F#m Em   A   D

Study Exercise   19   Arpeggios

C   Dm   Em   F   G Am Bm7(♭5) C   C   C Bm7(♭5) Am G   F   Em   Dm C   C

< 2 >

< 3 >

Study Exercise 29 6/8 Beat Tempo 68

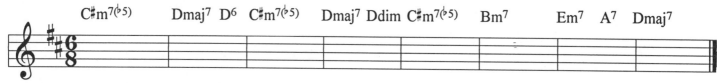

C#m7(b5)   Dmaj7 D6 C#m7(b5)   Dmaj7 Ddim C#m7(b5)   Bm7   Em7 A7 Dmaj7

Study Exercise 30 Rock Beat Tempo 130

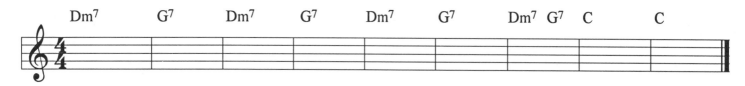

Dm7   G7   Dm7   G7   Dm7   G7   Dm7 G7 C   C

Study Exercise 31 16 Beat Feel Tempo 118

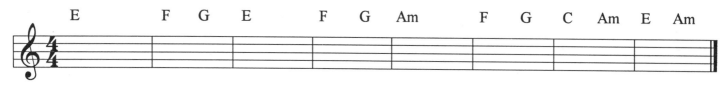

E   F   G   E   F   G   Am   F   G   C   Am   E   Am

Study Exercise 32 Hard Rock Tempo 122

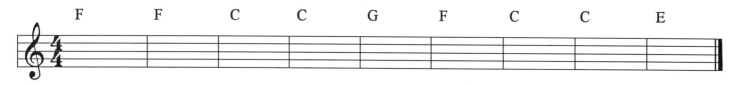

F   F   C   C   G   F   C   C   E

Study Exercise 33 Oldies Beat Tempo 178

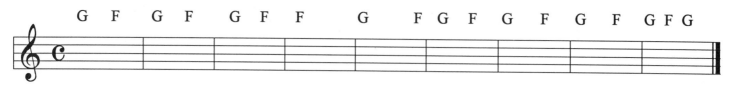

G   F   G   F   G   F   F   G   F G F G   F   G   F   G F G

Study Exercise 34 Brush Swing Tempo 122

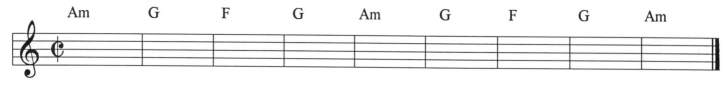

Am   G   F   G   Am   G   F   G   Am

Study Exercise 35 Lambada Tempo 126

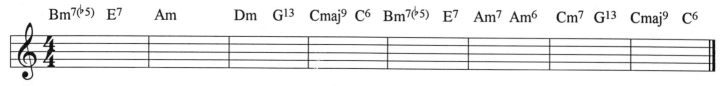

Bm7(b5) E7   Am   Dm G13 Cmaj9 C6 Bm7(b5) E7 Am7 Am6   Cm7 G13 Cmaj9 C6

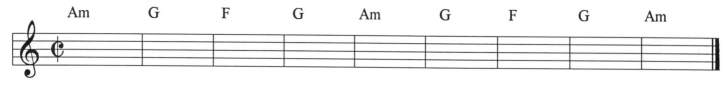

< 4 >

Study Exercise   36   Rhythm & Blues   Tempo   110

| Bm | Bm | A | A | Bm | Bm | A | A | A |

Study Exercise   37   Cha Cha   Tempo   124

| $C\sharp m^7$ | $Dmaj^7$ | Bm^7 E^7 | $C\sharp m$ $F\sharp m$ | Bm^7 E^7 | $Amaj^7$ A^7 | D $C\sharp m^7$ | Bm E^7 | A |

Study Exercise   38   Cajan Beat   Tempo   120

| D | A | E^7 | A A^7 | D | E | E^7 | A |

Study Exercise   39   Rock Beat   Tempo   155

| E^7 | A | A | Bm | Bm | E^7 | E^7 | E^7 | A | $Emaj^7$ | A |

Study Exercise   40   Rock Beat   Tempo   155

| $F\sharp m$ | Bm | $C\sharp$ | $F\sharp m$ | $F\sharp m$ | Bm | $C\sharp$ | $F\sharp$ | $F\sharp m$ |

Study Exercise   41   Rhumba Beat   Tempo   140

| E^7 | A^6 | $G\sharp m^{7(\flat5)}$ $C\sharp^7$ | $F\sharp m^7$ B^9 | Bm^7 E^7 | $Amaj^7$ $F\sharp m^7$ | Bm^7 E^7 | A $Amaj^7$ |

Study Exercise   42   Funk   Tempo   145

| Am | G | Am | C D Am | G | Am | C | Am |

Study Exercise   43   Pop Rock Tempo 124

Bm^7 Cmaj^7 D^{7}sus^4 D^7 Gmaj^7 G^6 Cmaj^7 Bm^7 Cmaj^7 D^7 Em^7 Am^7 D$^{7(\flat 9)}$ Gmaj^9

Study Exercise   44   Lambada Tempo 126

C   D   G   C   C   D   C   D   C   D   G

Study Exercise   45   Rock & Roll Ballad Tempo 134

G   Dsus^4 D Cmaj^7 D   G   Dsus^4 D   C G/B Am^7 Dsus^4 G

Study Exercise   46   Bossanova Tempo 150

Cmaj^7 Cmaj^9 Am^7 Am^7 D^{7}sus^4 D^7 Gmaj^7 Gmaj^7 Gmaj^7

Study Exercise   47   Swing Tempo 150

D^7 Bm^7 Em^7 Am^7 D^9 Gmaj^7 G^{13} Cmaj^7 Bm^7 Am^7 Gmaj^7 Cmaj^7 Bm^7 Cmaj^7 C/D G$^{6/9}$

Study Exercise   48   Rock Beat Tempo 155

F#^{5} B^5 F#^{5} C#^{5} F#^{5} B^5 F#^{5} C#^{5} F#^{5} F#^{5}

Study Exercise   49   Alternative Tempo 125

E   G#   C#m   Amaj^7 E   B^6 Amaj^7 B^6 C#m

< 6 >

Study Exercise 50 Country Waltz Tempo 122

A   A(add9)   F♯m   F♯m   B   B   A   A(add9)   E

Study Exercise 51 Hard Rock Tempo 121

B⁷sus⁴   B   E   F⁷sus⁴   B⁷sus⁴   B   E⁷sus⁴   E

Study Exercise 52 Beguine Tempo 140

C♯m   C♯m   G♯⁷   G♯⁷   C♯m   C♯m   F♯m   G♯m   C♯m⁹

Study Exercise 53 16 beat Tempo 77

Emaj⁹   Emaj⁹   C♯m⁹   C♯m⁹   F♯m⁹   F♯m⁷   B¹³⁽♭⁹⁾   E⁶ᐟ⁹

Study Exercise 54 Straight 4/4 Tempo 125

C

Study Exercise 55 Straight 44 Tempo 125

Dm

Study Exercise 56 Lambada Tempo 126

C   D   G   C   C D   C D   C D G

< 7 >

Study Exercise 57 Rock Beat   Tempo 130

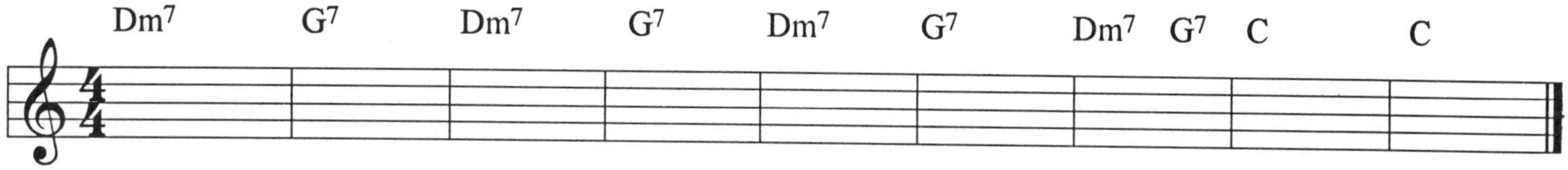

| Dm⁷ | G⁷ | Dm⁷ | G⁷ | Dm⁷ | G⁷ | Dm⁷ G⁷ C | C |

Study Exercise   58   6/8 Feel   Tempo 65

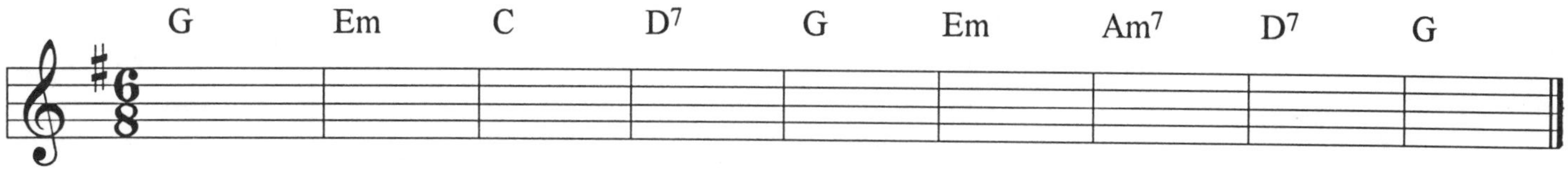

| G | Em | C | D⁷ | G | Em | Am⁷ | D⁷ | G |

Study Exercise 59 Country Shuffel Tempo 95

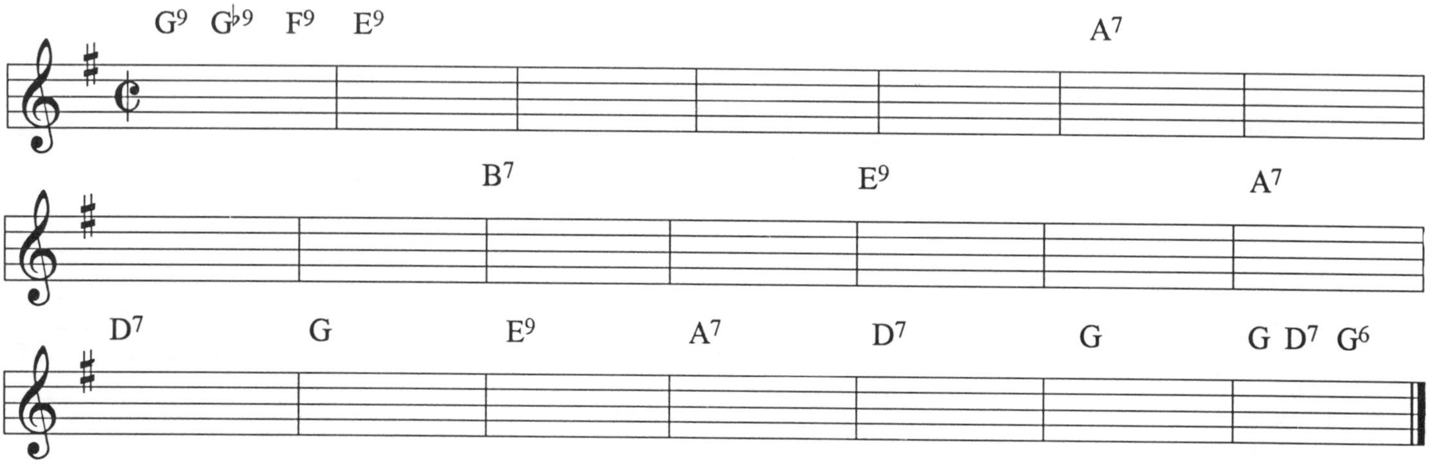

| G⁹ G♭⁹ F⁹ E⁹ | | | | | | A⁷ | |

| | B⁷ | | E⁹ | | A⁷ |

| D⁷ | G | E⁹ | A⁷ | D⁷ | G | G D⁷ G⁶ |

Study Exercise 60 Soul Ballad Tempo 105

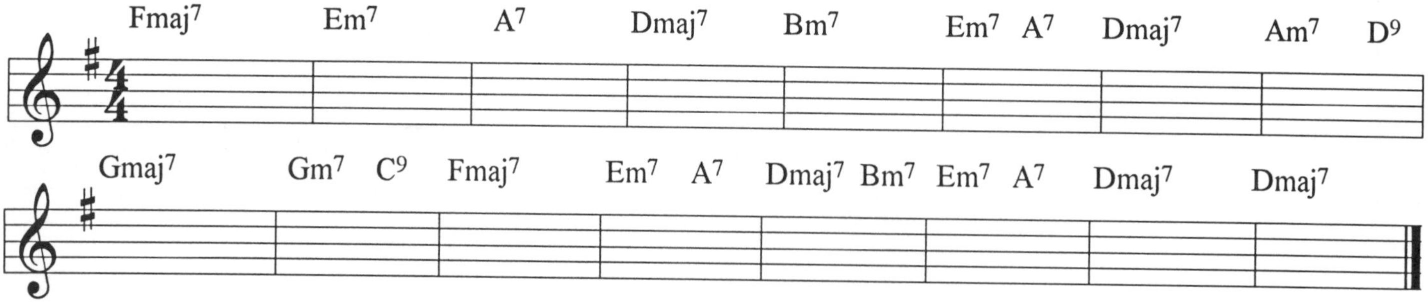

| Fmaj⁷ | Em⁷ | A⁷ | Dmaj⁷ | Bm⁷ | Em⁷ A⁷ | Dmaj⁷ | Am⁷ D⁹ |

| Gmaj⁷ | Gm⁷ C⁹ | Fmaj⁷ | Em⁷ A⁷ | Dmaj⁷ Bm⁷ | Em⁷ A⁷ | Dmaj⁷ | Dmaj⁷ |

Study Exercise 61 Swing Ballad Tempo 114

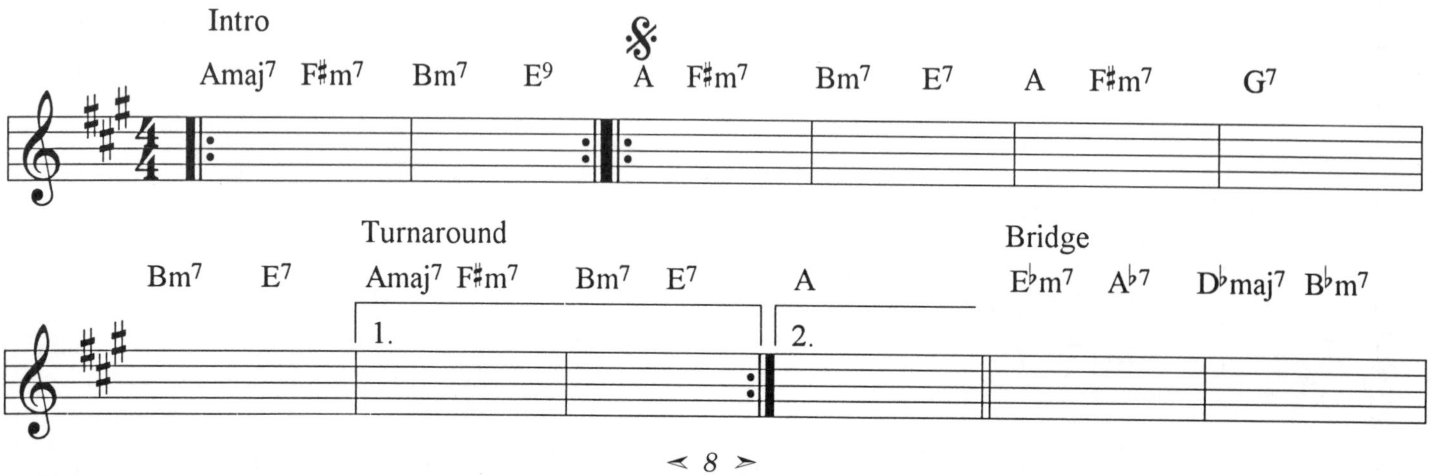

Intro

| Amaj⁷ F♯m⁷ | Bm⁷ E⁹ | 𝄋 A F♯m⁷ | Bm⁷ E⁷ | A F♯m⁷ | G⁷ |

Turnaround   Bridge

| Bm⁷ | E⁷ | 1. Amaj⁷ F♯m⁷ | Bm⁷ E⁷ | 2. A | E♭m⁷ A♭⁷ | D♭maj⁷ B♭m⁷ |

< 8 >

Study exercise 61 continued

E♭m⁷   A♭⁷   D♭maj⁷   D♭⁹   Em⁷   A⁷   Dmaj⁷   Bm⁷   Em⁷   A⁷   Dmaj⁷ D♯⁷ E⁷sus⁴

Verse
A   F♯m⁷   Bm⁷   E⁷   A   F♯m⁷   G⁹   Bm⁷ ⁻   E⁷   A   F♯m⁷

To Coda ⊕

Ending
Bm⁷   E⁷   Bm⁷   E⁷   A   F♯m⁷   Bm⁷   E⁷   A   B⁹   B♭⁹   A⁶ᐟ⁹

D.S. al Coda ⊕ ⊕

Fine

Study Exercise 62 Rock & Roll Tempo 120

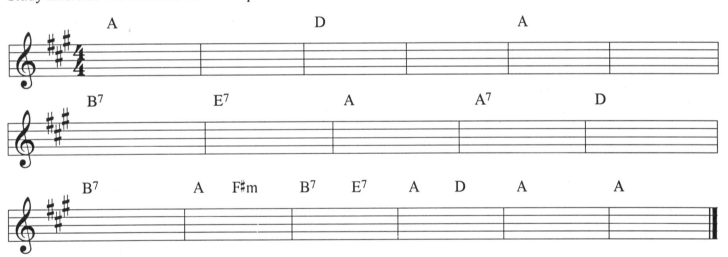

A   D   A

B⁷   E⁷   A   A⁷   D

B⁷   A   F♯m   B⁷   E⁷   A   D   A   A

Study Exercise 63 Country Tempo 85

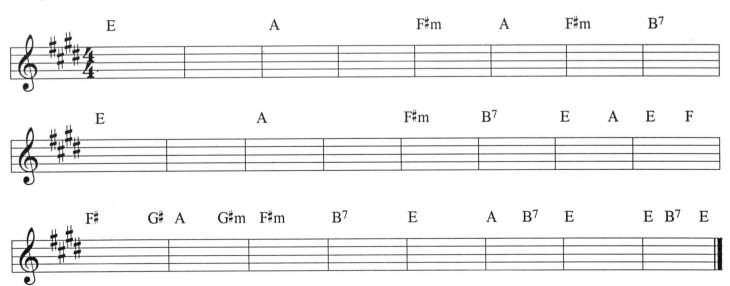

E   A   F♯m   A   F♯m   B⁷

E   A   F♯m   B⁷   E   A   E   F

F♯   G♯ A   G♯m F♯m   B⁷   E   A   B⁷   E   E B⁷ E

< 9 >

ROCK & ROLL SONG

Rock & Roll Song continued

COUNTRY SONG

< 11 >

Country Song continued

BLUES SONG

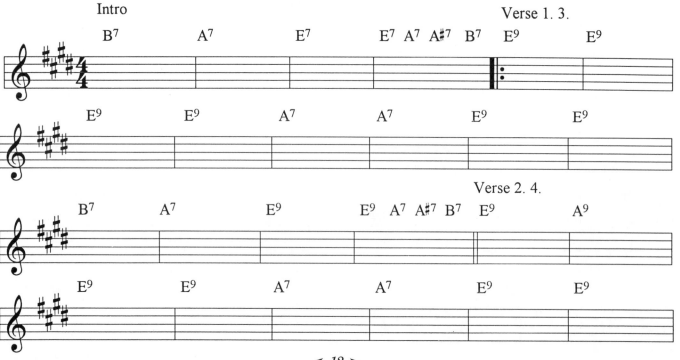

< *12* >

Blues Song continued

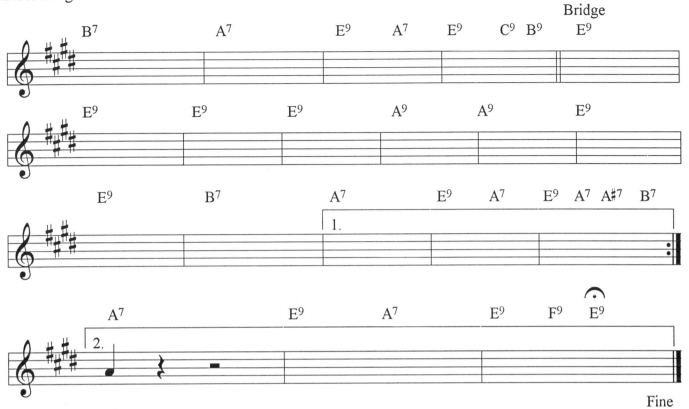

JAZZ SONG

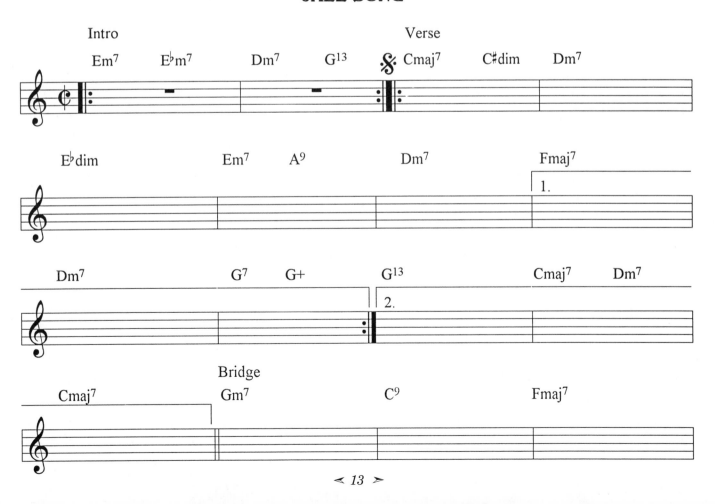

< 13 >

Jazz Song continued

< 14 >

CHORD DIAGRAMS

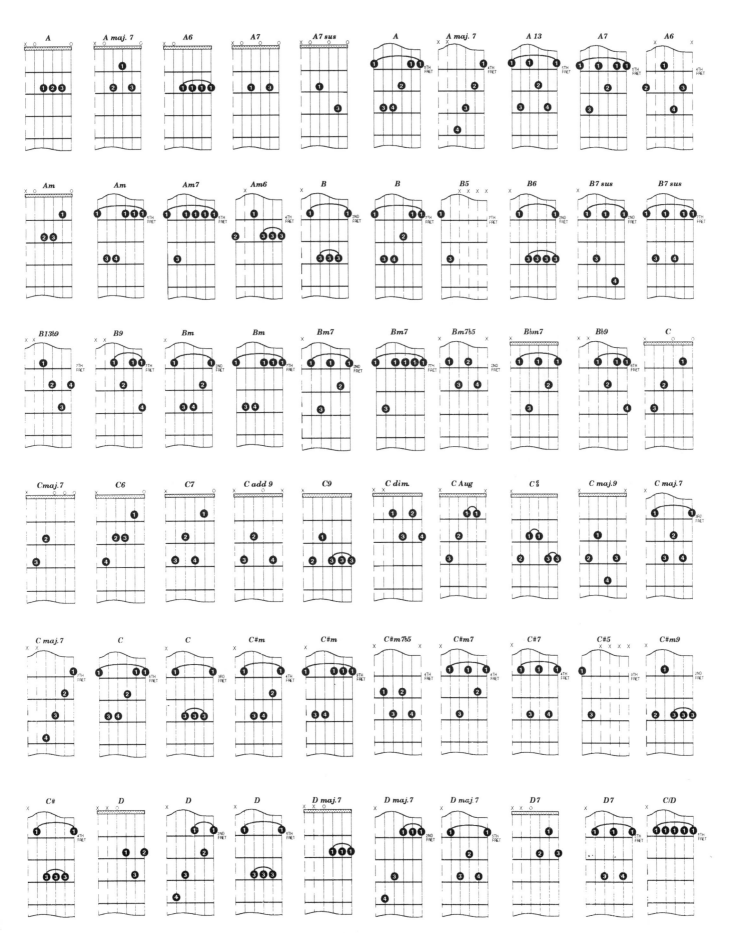

< 15 >

CHORD DIAGRAMS

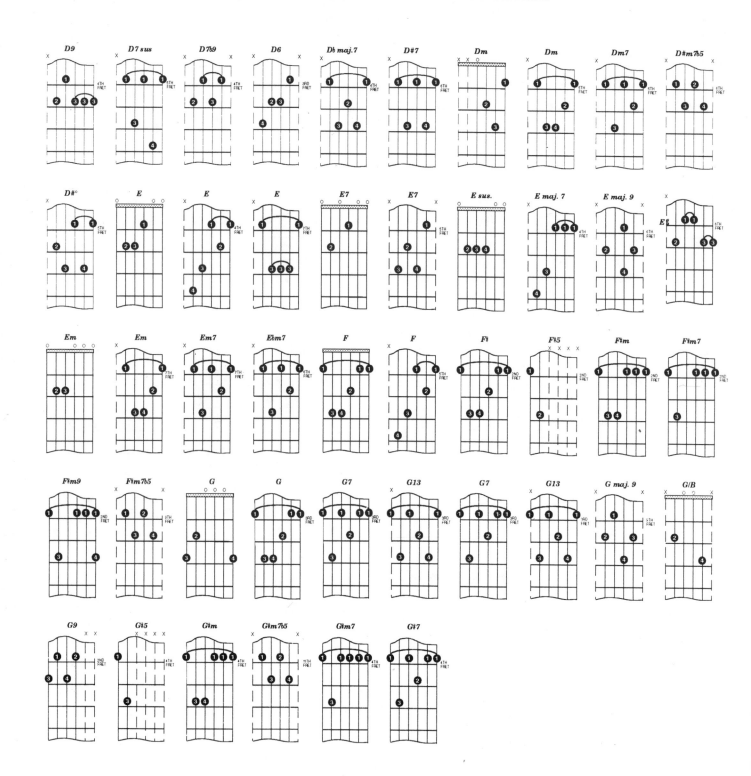